# QUILT-LOVERS' FAVORITES™

### FROM AMERICAN PATCHWORK & QUILTING®

Better Homes and Gardens® Creative Collection
Des Moines, Iowa

## VOLUME 1

Better Homes and Gardens®

# QUILT-LOVERS' FAVORITES™

FROM AMERICAN PATCHWORK & QUILTING®

Volume I

*Editor-in-Chief* BEVERLY RIVERS

## Quilt-Lovers' Favorites

| | |
|---|---|
| *Creative Director* | DANIEL MASINI |
| *Senior Editor* | EVE MAHR |
| *Associate Art Director* | CARRIE TOPP |
| *Contributing Editor* | JILL ABELOE MEAD |
| *Contributing Graphic Designer* | ERNIE SHELTON |
| *Administrative Assistant* | MARY JOHNSON |
| *Editorial Coordinator* | CAROL LINNAN |

## American Patchwork & Quilting

| | |
|---|---|
| *Department Head* JULIE KEITH | *Art Director* PATRICIA CHURCH PODLASEK |
| *Editor* | HEIDI KAISAND |
| *Project Editor* | JENNIFER KELTNER |
| *Associate Art Director* | MAUREEN MILLER |
| *Administrative Assistant* | MARY IRISH |
| *Contributing Copy Editors* | DIANE DORO, JENNIFER SPEER RAMUNDT, AND DEBRA MORRIS SMITH |
| *Quilt Tester* | LAURA BOEHNKE |
| *Technical Editor* | LILA SCOTT |
| *Contributing Illustrators* | MARCIA CAMERON, CHRIS NEUBAUER GRAPHICS |

| | |
|---|---|
| *Publishing Director* | WILLIAM R. REED |
| *Publisher* | MAUREEN RUTH |
| *Marketing Manager* | BECKY NASH |
| *Promotion Supervisor* | MERRI MOSER |
| *Business Manager* | CATHY BELLIS |
| *Production Director* | DOUGLAS M. JOHNSTON |
| *Book Production Managers* | PAM KVITNE, MARJORIE J. SCHENKELBERG |
| *Marketing Assistant* | MEGAN THOMPSON |

| | |
|---|---|
| *Vice President Publishing Director* | JERRY WARD |

| | |
|---|---|
| *Chairman and CEO* | WILLIAM T. KERR |
| *In Memoriam* | E.T. MEREDITH III (1933-2003) |

## Meredith Publishing Group

| | |
|---|---|
| *Publishing Group President* | STEPHEN M. LACY |
| *President, Magazine Group* | JERRY KAPLAN |
| *Creative Services* | ELLEN DE LATHOUDER |
| *Manufacturing* | BRUCE HESTON |
| *Consumer Marketing* | KARLA JEFFRIES |
| *Operations* | DEAN PIETERS |
| *Finance* | MAX RUNCIMAN |

Printed in China. First Edition.
Printing Number and Year: 5 4 3 2 1   04 03 02 01
ISBN: 0-696-21859-3

**For book editorial questions, write:**
*Better Homes and Gardens Quilt-Lovers' Favorites • 1716 Locust St., GA-305, Des Moines, IA 50309-3023*

# INSPIRED QUILTS

*I know you'll love this collection of quilt projects because, in a sense, you inspired it. The main projects in Quilt-Lovers' Favorites™ are all patterns regularly requested and tested by the readers of American Patchwork & Quilting® magazine. They are the projects that everyday readers, via letters, e-mails, and telephone calls, ask for. These also are the quilts I see in the snapshots that readers send me for the magazine's "Quilts & Quotes" section.*

*To accompany the 15 quilts pulled from the pages of our magazine, we've also generated brand-new projects using bits and pieces of the original quilts as inspiration. These easy-to-manage ideas are made in new color schemes to further spark your creativity. And, we added optional size charts where we could so you can make almost every quilt for any size bed you choose.*

*Enjoy these time-honored quilts—you know they're the Quilt-Lovers' Favorites.*

*Heidi Kaisand*

**Editor, American Patchwork & Quilting®**

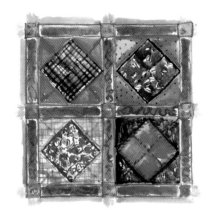

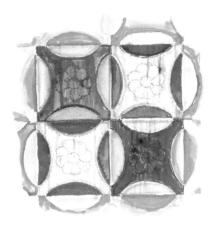

# TABLE of CONTENTS

*our*
## AGELESS HEIRLOOMS

*Page* **6**

*two-*
## COLOR TREASURES

*Page* **30**

*the*
# LOG CABIN
# COLLECTION
*Page* **60**

*the*
# INTERNATIONAL
# SPIRIT
*Page* **92**

*the*
# CHARM
*of* APPLIQUÉ
*Page* **118**

# our AGELESS HEIRLOOMS

Today's patchwork and quilting projects are rooted
in early American quilts. What we think of as
traditional patterns, such as Nine-Patch blocks,
emerged in the 1800s. These patterns were passed

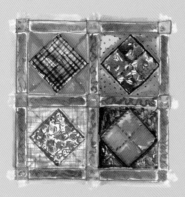 from one quilter to another until

they became embedded in the

American quilting tradition.

The quilts shown on the pages

that follow incorporate these textile

treasures and others, and will inspire 21st-century

quiltmakers to create their own family heirlooms.

# STORM *at* SEA

*"Although you get the impression of curved seams and motion when you first look at this quilt," notes designer Marti Michell, "the sense of curvature is achieved with straight seams that are sewn at slightly different angles to each other." Marti included a red heart in the lower right quadrant of this perennial favorite. For the most success, choose fabrics for the blocks that offer a high contrast between the background and the darkest print.*

## *the* QUILT

**Finished quilt top: 50½" square**
**Finished block: 10½" square**

Quantities specified for 44/45"-wide, 100% cotton fabrics. All measurements include a ¼" seam allowance unless otherwise stated.

### Cut the Fabrics

To make the best use of your fabrics, cut the pieces in the order that follows. Patterns for this project are on *Pattern Sheet 1*. To make templates of the patterns, follow the instructions in Quilter's Schoolhouse, which begins on *page 146*. The measurements for the border strips are mathematically correct. You may wish to cut your border strips longer than specified to allow for possible sewing differences.

### materials

1¾ yards of dark blue print for blocks, outer border, and binding

⅝ yard of blue print for blocks

⅓ yard of blue-and-white plaid for blocks

¼ yard of blue-and-white print for blocks

1½ yards of white print for blocks and flap

Scraps of dark red and red prints for blocks

¼ yard of dark red print for inner border

2⅜ yards of backing fabric

57" square of quilt batting

*continued*

From dark blue print, cut:
- 5—2¼×42" strips for outer border
- 5—2×42" binding strips
- 94 of Pattern C
- 33 of Pattern D

From blue print, cut:
- 62 of Pattern H

From blue-and-white plaid, cut:
- 16 of Pattern F

From blue-and-white print, cut:
- 25 of Pattern A

From white print, cut:
- 5—1×42" strips for flap
- 64 of Pattern G
- 100 of Pattern B
- 80 *each* of patterns E and E reversed

From dark red print scraps, cut:
- 7 of Pattern D

From red print scraps, cut:
- 2 of Pattern H
- 6 of Pattern C

From dark red print, cut:
- 5—1¼×42" strips for inner border

## Piece the Units

To avoid distorting the center of each unit, add the first two triangles to opposite edges, rather than working around the perimeter, and always press the seam allowances away from the center.

### Unit 1

1. Sew a white print B triangle to each edge of a blue-and-white print A square (see Diagram 1). Then add a dark blue print C triangle to each edge of the A/B unit to make a unit 1. Pieced unit 1 should measure 4" square, including the seam allowances. Repeat to make a total of 20 units.

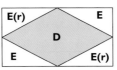
**Diagram 1**

2. Referring to the Quilt Assembly Diagram *opposite* for correct placement of the red pieces, also make four of unit 1 using three dark blue print C triangles and one red print C triangle and one of unit 1 with two dark blue print C triangles and two red print C triangles.

### Unit 2

1. Sew a white print E triangle to opposite edges of a dark blue print D diamond (see Diagram 2). Add a white print E reversed triangle to each remaining edge to make a unit 2. Pieced unit 2

**Diagram 2**

should measure 4×7½", including the seam allowances. Repeat to make a total of 33 of unit 2.

2. Repeat Step 1 to make seven of unit 2 using dark red print D diamonds.

### Unit 3

1. Sew a white print G triangle to each edge of a blue-and-white plaid F square (see Diagram 3). Then add a blue print H triangle to each edge of the F/G unit. Pieced unit 3 should measure 7½" square, including the seam allowances. Repeat to make a total of 14 units of unit 3.

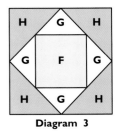
**Diagram 3**

2. Repeat Step 1 to make two of unit 3 using three blue print H triangles and one red print H triangle.

## Assemble the Storm at Sea Blocks

Each Storm at Sea block contains one of unit 1, two of unit 2, and one of unit 3. Twelve of the blocks are identical. The remaining four blocks contain red-accented units; see the Quilt Assembly Diagram for placement. Take special care to match the seams and triangular points when assembling the blocks, and later, when assembling the quilt center. Sew together the units in each block to make a total of 16 blocks. Each pieced block should measure 11" square, including the seam allowances.

## Assemble the Quilt Center

1. Lay out the blocks as shown in the Quilt Assembly Diagram, *opposite*. Sew together the blocks in rows. Press the seam allowances in each row in one direction, alternating direction with each row. Join the rows to complete the 16 block unit.

2. Join four of unit 1 and four of unit 2 to form the bottom strip (see the Quilt Assembly Diagram *opposite*). The bottom strip should measure 4×42½", including the seam allowances. Add the strip to the bottom edge of the 16 block unit.

3. Sew together five of Unit 1 and four of Unit 2 to form the side strip. Watch the placement of the red-accented units. The side strip should measure 4×46", including the seam allowances. Add the strip to the right hand edge of the 16 block unit to complete the quilt center.

## Add the Borders

1. Cut and piece the dark red print 1¼×42" strips into the following:
   - 2—1¼×46" inner border strips
   - 2—1¼×47½" inner border strips

2. Sew one short inner border strip to each side edge of the quilt center. Then add a long inner border strip to the top and bottom edges of the quilt center. Press the seam allowances toward the dark red print border strips.

3. The white print border is actually a flap (piping without a cord). Cut and piece the white print 1×42" strips into four 1×47½" strips. Press each strip in half lengthwise with wrong sides inside. Lay a strip along one side edge of the quilt center with raw edges matching; sew in place. Repeat on the opposite side edge, then on the top and bottom edges.

4. Cut and piece the dark blue print 2¼×42" strips into the following:
   - 2—2¼×47½" outer border strips
   - 2—2¼×51" outer border strips

5. Sew one short outer border strip to each side edge of the quilt center. Then add a long outer border strip to the top and bottom edges of the quilt center to complete the quilt top. Press the seam allowances toward the dark blue print outer border.

**Quilt Assembly Diagram**

## Complete the Quilt

Layer the quilt top, batting, and backing according to the instructions in Quilter's Schoolhouse, which begins on *page 146*. Quilt as desired. This quilt was quilted in the ditch. Use the dark blue print 2×42" strips to bind the quilt according to the instructions in Quilter's Schoolhouse.

---

## Storm at Sea Quilt

*optional sizes*

If you'd like to make this quilt in a size other than for a wall hanging, use the information *below*.

| Alternate Quilt Sizes | Twin | Full/Queen | King |
| --- | --- | --- | --- |
| **Number of blocks** | 28 | 48 | 49 |
| **Number of blocks wide by long** | 4×7 | 6×8 | 7×7 |
| **Border widths** | 3", 2", 5" | 3", 2", 5" | 4", 3", 6½" |
| **Finished size** | 56×87½" | 77×98" | 92½" square |
| | | | |
| **Yardage requirements** | | | |
| Dark blue print for blocks, outer border, and binding | 5½ yards | 8⅛ yards | 9⅛ yards |
| Blue print for blocks | 2⅛ yards | 3¼ yards | 3¼ yards |
| Blue-and-white plaid for blocks | ½ yard | ⅔ yard | ⅔ yard |
| Blue-and-white print for blocks | ¼ yard | ⅜ yard | ⅜ yard |
| White print for blocks and flap | 5⅞ yards | 9⅜ yards | 10¼ yards |
| Dark red print for heart and inner border | ¾ yard | ¾ yard | 1 yard |
| Backing | 5¼ yards | 5⅞ yards | 8¼ yards |
| Batting | 62×94" | 83×104" | 99" square |

## *the* HOLIDAY TABLE RUNNER

*Compose red-and-green Christmas print Storm at Sea blocks to make a runner that will dress your holiday table for years to come.*

### materials

½ yard of dark red print for blocks and inner border

¾ yard of dark red holly print for blocks

⅛ yard of poinsettia print for blocks

¾ yard of cream print for blocks

¼ yard of gold print for blocks and flap

½ yard of green print for borders and binding

1⅓ yards of backing fabric

26×48" of quilt batting

**Finished table runner top: 40½×19½"**

### Cut the Fabrics

To make best use of your fabrics, cut the pieces in the order that follows. This project uses "Storm at Sea" patterns, which are on *Pattern Sheet 1.* To make templates of the patterns, follow the instructions in Quilter's Schoolhouse, which begins on *page 146.* Measurements for the border strips are mathematically correct. You may wish to cut your border strips longer than specified to allow for possible sewing differences.

**From dark red print, cut:**
- 2—1¼×37" inner border strips
- 2—1¼×14½" inner border strips
- 8 of Pattern A
- 12 of Pattern H

**From dark red holly print, cut:**
- 10 of Pattern D
- 32 of Pattern C

**From poinsettia print, cut:**
- 3 of Pattern F

**From cream print, cut:**
- 20 *each* of patterns E and E reversed
- 12 of Pattern G

**From gold print, cut:**
- 2—¾×41" strips for flap
- 2—¾×20" strips for flap
- 32 of Pattern B

**From green print, cut:**
- 3—2½×42" binding strips
- 2—2½×41" outer border strips
- 2—2½×16" outer border strips

### Assemble the Units

**1.** For each unit 1 you'll need one dark red print A square, four gold print B triangles, and four dark red holly print C triangles. Referring to the Piece the Units instructions on *page 10,* make a total of eight of unit 1.

**2.** For each unit 2 you'll need one dark red holly print D diamond, two cream print E triangles, and two cream print E reversed triangles. Referring to the Piece the Units instructions on *page 10,* make a total of 10 of unit 2.

**3.** For each unit 3 you'll need one poinsettia print F square, four cream print G triangles, and four dark red print H triangles. Referring to the Piece the Units instructions on *page 10,* make a total of three of unit 3.

### Assemble the Table Runner

Referring to the photograph *opposite,* lay out the units in three horizontal rows; sew together in rows. Press the seam allowances in each row in one direction, alternating the direction with each row. Then join the rows to make the table runner center. The pieced table runner center should measure 35½×14½", including the seam allowances.

## Add the Borders

**I.** Sew a dark red print 1¼×14½" inner border strip to each side edge of the pieced table runner center. Then add a dark red print 1¼×37" inner border strip to the top and bottom edges of the pieced table runner center. Press all seam allowances toward the dark red print inner border.

**2.** Sew a green print 2½×16" outer border strip to each side edge of the pieced table runner center. Then add a green print 2½×41" outer border strip to the top and bottom edges of the pieced table runner center. Press all seam allowances toward the green print outer border.

**3.** The gold print border is actually a flap (piping without a cord). Fold the gold print ¾×20" strips in half lengthwise with the wrong sides inside; press. Lay a flap strip along one short edge of the pieced table runner center with raw edges matching; sew in place. Repeat on the opposite short edge.

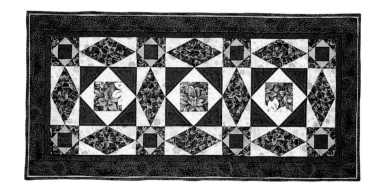

**4.** Fold the gold print ¾×41" strips in half lengthwise; press. Sew the strips to the long edges of the pieced table runner center to complete the table runner top.

## Complete the Table Runner

Layer the table runner top, batting, and backing according to the instructions in Quilter's Schoolhouse, which begins on *page 146*. Quilt as desired. This quilt was outline-quilted by machine with gold metallic thread. Use the green print 2½×42" strips to bind the quilt according to the instructions in Quilter's Schoolhouse.

# *the* TABLETOP QUILT

*For a quick-to-make tabletop quilt we bordered a square of autumn-inspired fabric with two of the Storm at Sea units.*

## materials

1⅛ yards of fall-theme print for quilt center

⅔ yard of dark green print for inner border and binding

⅓ yard of brown print for units

⅛ yard of dark gold print for units

¼ yard of solid gold for units

½ yard of red print for units

½ yard of gold print for units

2¼ yards of backing fabric

52" square of quilt batting

**Finished quilt top: 45½" square**

## Cut the Fabrics

To make the best use of your fabrics, cut the pieces in the order that follows. This project uses "Storm at Sea" patterns, which are on *Pattern Sheet 1*. To make templates of the patterns, follow the instructions in Quilter's Schoolhouse, which begins on *page 146*. The measurements for the border strips are mathematically correct. You may wish to cut the border strips longer than specified to allow for possible sewing differences.

**From fall-theme print, cut:**
- 1—36½" square for center

**From dark green print, cut:**
- 5—2½×42" binding strips
- 2—1¾×39" inner border strips
- 2—1¾×36½" inner border strips

**From brown print, cut:**
- 64 of Pattern C

**From dark gold print, cut:**
- 16 of Pattern A

**From solid gold, cut:**
- 64 of Pattern B

**From red print, cut:**
- 32 *each* of patterns E and E reversed

**From gold print, cut:**
- 16 of Pattern D

## Add the Inner Border

Sew a dark green print 1¾×36½" inner border strip to each side edge of the fall-theme print 36½" square. Then add a dark green print 1¾×39" inner border strip to the top and bottom edges of the fall-theme print 36½" square to make the quilt center. Press all seam allowances toward the dark green print inner border.

## Assemble the Units

1. For each unit 1 you'll need one dark gold print A square, four solid gold B triangles, and four brown print C triangles. Referring to the Piece the Units instructions on *page 10*, make a total of 16 of unit 1.

2. For each unit 2 you'll need one gold print D diamond, two red print E triangles, and two red print E reversed triangles. Referring to the Piece the Units instructions on *page 10* make a total of 16 of unit 2.

## Assemble and Add the Pieced Border

1. Lay out four of unit 2 and three of unit 1 in a row, alternating the units; sew together to make a border strip. Press the seam allowances in one direction. The pieced border strip should measure 4×39", including the seam allowances. Repeat to make a total of four border strips.

2. Sew a pieced border strip to each side edge of the quilt center.

3. Sew one unit 1 to each end of the two remaining pieced border strips.

4. Sew the remaining pieced border strips to the top and bottom edges of the quilt center. Press the seam allowances toward the dark green print border.

## Complete the Quilt

Layer the quilt top, batting, and backing according to the instructions in Quilter's Schoolhouse, which begins on *page 146*. Quilt as desired. This quilt was machine-quilted with an Oak Branch Quilting Design in the center section (see *Pattern Sheet 1*); the pieced borders were quilted in the ditch. Use the dark green print 2½×42" strips to bind the quilt according to the instructions in Quilter's Schoolhouse.

---

# *the* BABY QUILT

*Nothing says sweetness like this fresh blue, white, and yellow baby quilt. We raided the scrap box for a sampling of blue and yellow prints to make the two units from "Storm at Sea."*

**Finished quilt top: 39" square**

## Cut the Fabrics

To make the best use of your fabrics, cut the pieces in the order that follows. This project uses "Storm at Sea" patterns, which are on *Pattern Sheet 1*. To make templates of the patterns, follow the instructions in Quilter's Schoolhouse, which begins on *page 146*. The measurements for the border strips are

## materials

16—⅛-yard pieces of assorted yellow prints
    for blocks

¼ yard of light blue dot for blocks

9—⅛-yard pieces of blue prints for blocks

¾ yard of yellow dot for blocks and binding

¾ yard of yellow-and-white print for sashing

⅓ yard of blue-and-yellow print for borders

1¼ yards of backing fabric

45" square of quilt batting

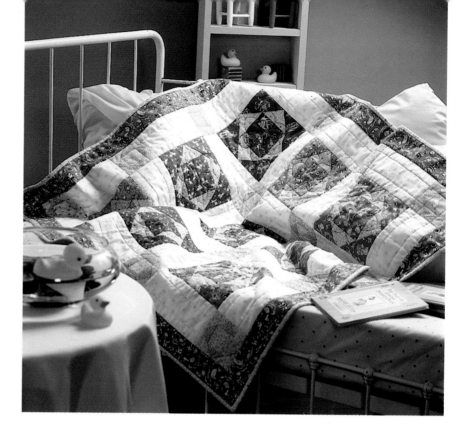

mathematically correct. You may wish to cut your border strips longer than specified to allow for possible sewing differences.

From *each* of the 16 assorted yellow prints, cut:
- 1 of Pattern A
- 4 of Pattern C

From light blue dot, cut:
- 64 of Pattern B

From *each* of the 9 assorted blue prints, cut:
- 1 of Pattern F
- 4 of Pattern H

From yellow dot, cut:
- 4—2½×42" binding strips
- 36 of Pattern G

From yellow-and-white print, cut:
- 24—4×7½" rectangles for sashing

From blue-and-yellow print, cut:
- 2—2½×39½" border strips
- 2—2½×35½" border strips

## Assemble the Units

1. For each unit 1 you'll need one assorted yellow print A square, four light blue dot B triangles, and four assorted yellow print C triangles. Referring to the Piece the Units instructions on *page 10*, make a total of 16 of unit 1.

2. For each unit 3 you'll need one assorted blue print F square, four yellow dot G triangles, and four assorted blue print H triangles. Referring to the Piece the Units instructions on *page 10*, make a total of nine of unit 3.

## Assemble the Quilt Center

1. Referring to the photograph *above,* lay out the 16 of unit 1, the nine of unit 3, and the 24 yellow-and-white print 4×7½" sashing rectangles in seven horizontal rows.

2. Sew together the pieces in each row. Press the seam allowances toward the yellow-and-white print sashing rectangles. Then join the rows to complete the quilt center. Press the seam allowances in one direction. The pieced quilt center should measure 35½" square, including the seam allowances.

## Add the Border

Sew one blue-and-yellow print 2½×35½" border strip to the top and bottom edges of the pieced quilt center. Then join one blue-and-yellow print 2½×39½" border strip to each side edge of the pieced quilt center to complete the quilt top. Press all seam allowances toward the outer border.

## Complete the Quilt

Layer the quilt top, batting, and backing according to the instructions in Quilter's Schoolhouse, which begins on *page 146*. Quilt as desired. This quilt was machine-quilted with a Looped Medallion Quilting Design in the center of each large unit (see *Pattern Sheet 1*); straight lines were stitched on the sashing strips and small units. Use the yellow dot 2½×42" strips to bind the quilt according to the instructions in Quilter's Schoolhouse.

# CONVENT QUILT

*When a group of Quebec nuns received scraps of shirting*

*fabric around the turn of the 20th century, they set right to quilting.*

*More than 90 years later, 102 traditional Nine-Patch quilts were discovered*

*in their convent. "These quilts epitomize a convent," antiques dealer*

*John Sauls says. "The nuns did not waste anything they were given,*

*and the quilts served dual purposes. They learned to quilt on these pieces*

*that would then serve as blankets to keep them warm."*

*the* QUILT

## materials

2¼ yards total of assorted shirting stripes for
    setting squares

1⅝ yards total of assorted blue prints for blocks

1½ yards of muslin for blocks

½ yard of blue-and-white stripe for binding

3½ yards of backing fabric

60×90" of quilt batting

**Finished quilt top: 54×81"**
**Finished block: 6¾" square**

Quantities specified for 44/45"-wide, 100% cotton
fabrics. All measurements include a ¼" seam
allowance unless otherwise stated.

### Cut the Fabrics

To make the best use of your fabrics, cut the pieces
in the order that follows.

From assorted shirting stripes, cut:
• 48—7¼" squares for setting

From assorted blue prints, cut:
• 18—2¾×42" strips

From muslin, cut:
• 15—2¾×42" strips

From blue-and-white stripe, cut:
• 7—2×42" binding strips

*continued*

## Assemble the Nine-Patch Blocks

1. Aligning long edges, sew two blue print 2¾×42" strips to a muslin 2¾×42" strip to make a strip set A (see Diagram 1). Press the seam allowances toward the blue print strips. Repeat to make a total of seven of strip set A. Cut the strip sets into 2¾"-wide segments for a total of 96.

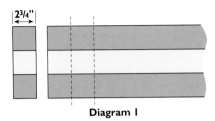

**Diagram 1**

2. Aligning long edges, sew two muslin 2¾×42" strips to a blue print 2¾×42" strip to make a strip set B (see Diagram 2). Press the seam allowances toward the blue print strip. Repeat to make a total of four of strip set B. Cut the strip sets into 2¾"-wide segments for a total of 48.

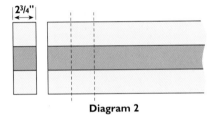

**Diagram 2**

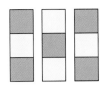

**Diagram 3**

3. Sew together two strip set A segments and one strip set B segment to make a Nine-Patch block (see Diagram 3). Press the seam allowances toward the center segment. The Nine-Patch block should measure 7¼" square, including seam allowances. Repeat to make a total of 48 Nine-Patch blocks.

## Assemble the Quilt Top

1. Lay out the 48 Nine-Patch blocks and the 48 assorted shirting stripe 7¼" setting squares in 12 horizontal rows with four blocks and four setting squares in each row. Alternate the position of blocks and setting squares with each row.

2. Join the blocks and setting squares in each row. Press the seam allowances toward the setting squares. Then sew together the rows to complete the quilt top. Press the seam allowances in one direction.

## Complete the Quilt

Layer the quilt top, batting, and backing according to the instructions in Quilter's Schoolhouse, which begins on *page 146*. Quilt as desired. This quilt was hand-quilted in a crosshatch pattern. Use the blue-and-white stripe 2×42" strips to bind the quilt according to the instructions in Quilter's Schoolhouse.

## Convent Quilt
### *optional sizes*

If you'd like to make this quilt in a size other than for a single bed, use the information *below*.

| Alternate Quilt Sizes | Crib/Lap | Full/Queen | King |
|---|---|---|---|
| **Number of Nine-Patch blocks** | 24 | 84 | 128 |
| **Number of setting squares** | 24 | 84 | 128 |
| **Number of blocks wide by long** | 6×8 | 12×14 | 16×16 |
| **Finished size** | 40½×54" | 81×94½" | 108" square |
| | | | |
| **Yardage requirements** | | | |
| Shirting stripes | 1¼ yards | 3 yards | 4½ yards |
| Blue prints | 1 yard | 2½ yards | 3⅝ yards |
| Muslin | ¾ yard | 2 yards | 3 yards |
| Blue-and-white stripe for binding | ⅓ yard | ⅝ yard | ⅔ yard |
| Backing | 1¾ yards | 5⅝ yards | 9½ yards |
| Quilt batting | 47×60" | 87×100" | 114" square |

# optional colors

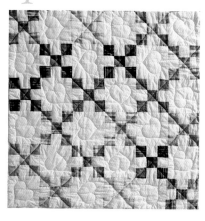 

## Convent Quilt Color Options

Our color options show two different schemes for the "Convent Quilt." Plaid scraps and muslin squares compose the Nine-Patch blocks in the option *far left*. Setting squares in two different colors create a new pattern in the quilt *at left*.

# *the* '30s THROW

*Reproductions of printed fabrics from the '30s give this lap quilt its vintage charm.*

## materials

- 1¼ yards of light tan print for setting squares and inner border
- 13—4½×18" (fat eighth) pieces of assorted light pastel prints for blocks and border
- 13—4½×18" (fat eighth) pieces of assorted dark pastel prints for blocks and border
- ½ yard of dark green print for blocks and binding
- 2¾ yards of backing fabric
- 49" square of quilt batting

**Finished quilt top: 42¾" square**

*continued*

## Cut the Fabrics

To make the best use of your fabrics, cut the pieces in the order that follows.

From light tan print, cut:
- 2—2¾×38¾" inner border strips
- 2—2¾×34¼" inner border strips
- 12—7¼" squares for setting

From *each* assorted light pastel print, cut:
- 7—2¾" squares

From *each* assorted dark pastel print, cut:
- 7—2¾" squares

From dark green print, cut:
- 5—2½×42" binding strips
- 13—2¾" squares

## Assemble the Nine-Patch Blocks

1. Referring to the Block Assembly Diagram, lay out four matching light pastel print 2¾" squares, four matching dark pastel print 2¾" squares, and one dark green print 2¾" square in three horizontal rows.

**Block Assembly Diagram**

2. Sew together the squares in each row. Press the seam allowances toward the darker squares. Then join the rows to make a Nine-Patch block. Press the seam allowances in one direction. The pieced block should measure 7¼" square, including the seam allowances.

3. Repeat steps 1 and 2 to make a total of 13 Nine-Patch blocks.

## Assemble the Quilt Center

1. Referring to the photograph *above,* lay out the 13 Nine-Patch blocks and 12 light tan print 7¼" setting squares in five horizontal rows.

2. Sew together the Nine-Patch blocks and setting squares in each row. Press the seam allowances toward the setting squares. Then join the rows to make the quilt center. Press the seam allowances in one direction. The pieced quilt center should measure 34¼" square, including the seam allowances.

## Add the Borders

1. Sew a light tan print 2¾×34¼" inner border strip to the top and bottom edges of the pieced quilt center. Then add a light tan print 2¾×38¾" inner border strip to each side edge of the pieced quilt center. Press all seam allowances toward the light tan print border.

2. Sew together 17 assorted light and dark pastel print 2¾" squares in a row to make the top outer border strip. The pieced top outer border strip should measure 2¾×38¾", including the seam allowances. Repeat to make the bottom outer border strip. Join the top and bottom outer border strips to the top and bottom edges of the pieced quilt center.

3. Sew together 19 assorted light and dark pastel print 2¾" squares in a row to make a side outer border strip. The pieced side outer border strip should measure 2¾×43¼", including the seam allowances. Repeat to make a second side outer border strip. (There should be six leftover assorted pastel print squares.) Join the side outer border strips to the side edges of the pieced quilt center to complete the quilt top.

## Complete the Quilt

Layer the quilt top, batting, and backing according to the instructions in Quilter's Schoolhouse, which begins on *page 146.* Quilt as desired. This quilt was machine-quilted with a Floral Pinwheel Quilting Design in each pieced square and a Circular Leaf Quilting Design (see *Pattern Sheet 1*) in each setting square. Use the dark green print 2½×42" strips to bind the quilt according to the instructions in Quilter's Schoolhouse.

# the PATRIOTIC TABLE RUNNER

*Stand up and cheer for this red, white, and blue version of the "Convent Quilt."*

## materials

½ yard of dark blue print for setting squares

½ yard of red print for blocks and binding

¼ yard of light tan print for blocks

¾ yard of backing fabric

27×40" square of quilt batting

**Finished table runner top: 33¾×20¼"**

## Cut the Fabrics

To make the best use of your fabrics, cut the pieces in the order that follows:

From dark blue print, cut:
• 8—7¼" squares for setting

From red print, cut:
• 3—2¾×42" strips
• 3—2½×42" binding strips

From light tan print, cut:
• 3—2¾×42" strips

## Assemble the Nine-Patch Blocks

Refer to the Assemble the Nine-Patch Blocks instructions on *page 18* for more details on the following steps.

1. Make one strip set A by sewing two red print 2¾×42" strips to a light tan 2¾×42" print strip. Cut the strip set into fourteen 2¾"-wide segments.

2. Make one strip set B by sewing two light tan print 2¾×42" strips to a red print 2¾×42" strip. Cut the strip set into seven 2¾" segments.

3. Sew together two strip set A segments and one strip set B segment to make a Nine-Patch block. The pieced Nine-Patch block should measure 7¼" square, including the seam allowances. Repeat to make a total of seven Nine-Patch blocks.

## Assemble the Table Runner

1. Referring to the photograph *below* for placement, lay out the seven Nine-Patch blocks and the eight dark blue print 7¼" setting squares in three horizontal rows.

2. Join the blocks and setting squares in each row. Press the seam allowances toward the setting squares. Then sew together the rows to make the table runner top. Press the seam allowances in one direction.

## Complete the Table Runner

Layer the table runner top, batting, and backing according to the instructions in Quilter's Schoolhouse, which begins on *page 146*. Quilt as desired. In this quilt, the square pieces in each block were outline-quilted by machine. The setting squares were quilted with red thread and a meandering squiggles and stars pattern. Use the red print 2½×42" strips to bind the quilt according to the instructions in Quilter's Schoolhouse.

# TOWN SQUARE

*Designer Marjorie Levine relied on the wide assortment of reproduction*

*fabrics in her stash to create this antique-looking Town Square quilt.*

*Marjorie pieced as the quilters of the past would have worked—without specific*

*rules for combining a variety of prints. She would dip her hand into her*

*scrap bag, pull out two fabrics, and combine them into a block.*

*Change the colors in this design and you will create an entirely fresh look, as is*

*evidenced in the tablecloth, wall hanging, and pillowcase that follow.*

## *the* QUILT

### materials

1¾ yards total of assorted light, medium, and dark

 prints for blocks

1⅝ yards of brown stripe for sashing and binding

⅜ yard of pink-and-gold print for sashing squares

¾ yard of brown print for border

3 yards of backing fabric

52×62" of quilt batting

**Finished quilt top: 47¼×56¾"**
**Finished block: 3½" square**

Quantities specified for 44/45"-wide, 100% cotton fabrics. All measurements include a ¼" seam allowance unless otherwise stated.

### Cut the Fabrics
To make the best use of your fabrics, cut the pieces in the order that follows.

From assorted light, medium, and dark prints, cut:
- 80—3" squares for block centers
- 80 sets of 2—2⅝" squares; cut each square in half diagonally for a total of 4 corner triangles in each set

From brown stripe, cut:
- 6—2½×42" binding strips
- 178—1¾×4" sashing strips

From pink-and-gold print, cut:
- 99—1¾" squares for sashing

From brown print, cut:
- 5—4½×42" border strips

*continued*

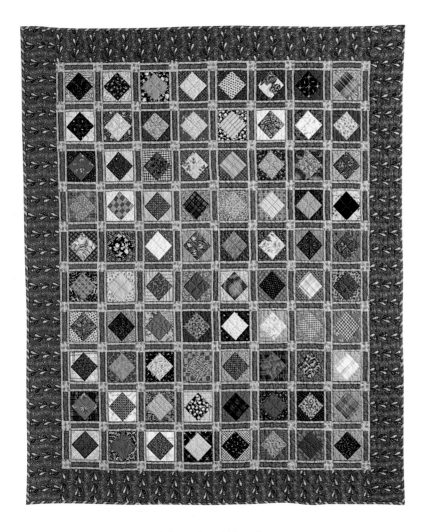

Our Ageless Heirlooms

## Assemble the Blocks

**1.** For one block you'll need one 3" square and one contrasting set of four corner triangles.

**2.** With right sides together, align the long edge of a triangle with one edge of the square (see Diagram 1). Sew together the pieces. Press the seam allowance toward the triangle. In the same manner, align a second triangle with the opposite edge of the square; join and press the seam allowance.

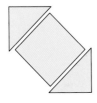   

**Diagram I**          **Diagram 2**

**3.** Add the remaining two triangles to the square's remaining raw edges in the same manner (see Diagram 2). The pieced block should measure 4" square, including the seam allowances.

**4.** Repeat steps 1 through 3 to make a total of 80 blocks.

## Assemble the Rows

**1.** Lay out eight pieced blocks and nine brown stripe 1¾×4" sashing strips in a horizontal row, alternating them and beginning and ending the row with a sashing strip. Join the pieces to make a block row. The pieced block row should measure 4×39¾", including the seam allowances. Repeat to make a total of 10 block rows.

**2.** Lay out nine pink-and-gold 1¾" sashing squares and eight brown stripe 1¾×4" sashing strips in a horizontal row, alternating them and beginning and ending the row with a sashing square. Join the pieces to make a sashing row. The pieced sashing row should measure 1¾×39¾", including seam allowances. Repeat to make a total of 11 sashing rows.

## Assemble the Quilt Center

Referring to the photograph at *left* for placement, lay out the sashing and block rows. Alternate the rows, beginning and ending with a sashing row. Join the rows to make the quilt center. The pieced quilt center should measure 39¾×49¼", including the seam allowances.

## Add the Border

**1.** Cut and piece the brown print 4½×42" border strips to make the following:
- 2—4½×39¾" border strips
- 2—4½×57¼" border strips

**2.** Sew one short border strip to the top and bottom edges of the pieced quilt center. Then join a long border strip to each side edge of the pieced quilt center to complete the quilt top. Press all seam allowances toward the brown print border.

## Complete the Quilt

Layer the quilt top, batting, and backing according to the instructions in Quilter's Schoolhouse, which begins on *page 146*. Quilt as desired. This quilt was hand-quilted in a 1¼"-wide diagonal grid. Use the brown stripe 2½×42" strips to bind the quilt according to the instructions in Quilter's Schoolhouse.

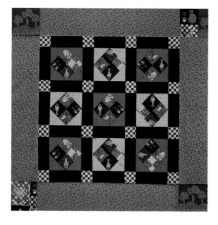  

## Three Times the Fun

The versatility of the block in "Town Square" makes experimenting with colors fun. For example, *above from left*, cat-motif fabrics make a whimsical variation; solids create an Amish-style coloration, and pinks, roses, plums, and blues offer a cheerful rendition.

## Town Square Quilt

*optional sizes*

If you'd like to make this quilt in a size other than for a lap quilt, use the information *below*.

| Alternate Quilt Sizes | Twin | Full | Queen | King |
|---|---|---|---|---|
| **Number of blocks** | 144 | 285 | 336 | 441 |
| **Number of blocks wide by long** | 9×16 | 15×19 | 16×21 | 21×21 |
| **Finished size** | 52×85¼" | 80½×99½" | 85¼×109" | 109" square |
| | | | | |
| **Yardage requirements** | | | | |
| Assorted light, medium and dark prints for blocks | 2⅝ yards | 4⅜ yards | 5⅝ yards | 7½ yards |
| Brown stripe for sashing and binding | 2¼ yards | 3¾ yards | 4¼ yards | 5⅜ yards |
| Pink-and-gold print for sashing squares | ½ yard | ¾ yard | ⅞ yard | 1⅛ yards |
| Brown print for border | 1¼ yards | 1⅜ yards | 1½ yards | 1⅝ yards |
| Backing | 5 yards | 7¼ yards | 7⅔ yards | 9⅝ yards |
| Batting | 58×92" | 88×106" | 92×115" | 115" square |

*the*
# AMISH WALL HANGING

*Solid-color fabrics compose this Amish-style wall hanging. Unlike the original "Town Square" quilt, this project requires careful planning of color placement.*

## materials

Scraps of nine assorted solid jewel tones for blocks

⅓ yard of solid black for setting squares

⅜ yard of solid rust for sashing and binding

¼ yard of solid magenta for border

¾ yard of backing fabric

27" square of quilt batting

*continued*

**Finished quilt top: 20½" square**

## Cut the Fabrics

To make the best use of your fabrics, cut the pieces in the order that follows.

From *each* of nine assorted solid jewel tones, cut:
• 1—3" square for block center

From solid black, cut:
• 18—2⅝" squares, cutting each in half diagonally for a total of 36 corner triangles
• 4—3" squares for border
• 16—1¾" squares for sashing

From solid rust, cut:
• 3—2½×42" binding strips
• 24—1¾×4" sashing strips

From solid magenta, cut:
• 4—3×16" border strips

## Assemble the Blocks

Referring to the Assemble the Blocks instructions on *page 24*, use one solid jewel-tone 3" square and four solid black corner triangles to make a block. Repeat to make a total of nine blocks.

## Assemble the Rows

1. Lay out three pieced blocks and four solid rust sashing strips in a horizontal row, alternating them and beginning and ending the row with a sashing strip. Join the pieces to make a block row. The pieced block row should measure 4×16", including the seam allowances. Repeat to make a total of three block rows.

2. Lay out four solid black 1¾" sashing squares and three solid rust 1¾×4" sashing strips in a horizontal row, alternating them and beginning and ending the row with a sashing square. Join the pieces to make a sashing row. The pieced sashing row should measure 1¾×16", including the seam allowances. Repeat to make a total of four sashing rows.

## Assemble the Quilt Center

Referring to the photograph *at left* for placement, lay out the sashing and block rows. Alternate the rows, beginning and ending with a sashing row. Join the rows to make the quilt center. The pieced quilt center should measure 16" square, including the seam allowances.

## Add the Border

1. Sew one solid magenta 3×16" border strip to each side edge of the pieced quilt center. Press the seam allowances toward the border.

2. Join one solid black corner 3" square to each end of the remaining solid magenta 3×16" border strips. Press the seam allowance toward the solid magenta strips. Then sew a pieced border strip to the top and bottom edges of the quilt center to complete the quilt top. Press the seam allowances toward the border.

## Complete the Quilt

Layer the quilt top, batting, and backing according to the instructions in Quilter's Schoolhouse, which begins on *page 146*. Quilt as desired. This wall hanging was machine-quilted with black thread. Pieced blocks were quilted in a diagonal grid and the borders with a scroll design. Use the solid rust 2½×42" strips to bind the quilt according to the instructions in Quilter's Schoolhouse.

# *the* PICNIC TABLECLOTH

*This cheerful picnic cloth in all-American colors brightens any location. Add rows of blocks and sashing to change the size to fit your table.*

**Finished quilt top: 42" square**
**Finished block: 6" square**

## Cut the Fabrics

To make the best use of your fabrics, cut the pieces in the order that follows.

From red print, cut:
- 25—3" squares for block centers

From red-and-white print, cut:
- 50—2⅝" squares, cutting each in half diagonally for a total of 100 corner triangles
- 100—1¾" squares for sashing

From blue print, cut:
- 100—1¾×4" sashing strips

From red check, cut:
- 5—2½×42" binding strips
- 24—6½" setting squares

## materials

¼ yard of red print for blocks

⅝ yard of red-and-white print for blocks and
  sashing squares

⅝ yard of blue print for sashing

1½ yards of red check for setting squares and binding

2⅔ yards of backing fabric

*continued*

## Assemble the Blocks

1. Referring to the Assemble the Blocks instructions on *page 24*, use one red print 3" square and four red-and-white print corner triangles to make a block. Repeat to make a total of 25 blocks.

2. Sew one blue print 1¾×4" sashing strip to each side edge of each block. Press the seam allowances toward the sashing strips.

3. Join one red-and-white print 1¾" sashing square to each end of the remaining sashing strips. Then sew a pieced sashing strip to the top and bottom edges of the blocks. Press the seam allowances toward the sashing strips. Each block should now measure 6½" square, including the seam allowances.

## Assemble the Quilt Top

1. Lay out the blocks and red check 6½" setting squares in seven horizontal rows. Odd-numbered rows should have four blocks and three setting squares. Even-numbered rows should have four setting squares and three blocks. Alternate the position of blocks and setting squares within each row.

2. Join the blocks and the setting squares in each row. Press the seam allowances toward the setting squares. Then sew together the rows to complete the quilt top. Press the seam allowances in one direction.

## Complete the Quilt

Layer the quilt top, batting, and backing according to the instructions in Quilter's Schoolhouse, which begins on *page 146*. This tablecloth was machine-quilted following the seam lines of the block sashing. Use the red check 2½×42" strips to bind the quilt according to the instructions in Quilter's Schoolhouse.

# *the* PILLOWCASE

*A border of Town Square blocks marches 'round the opening of this decorative pillowcase. Select your favorite coordinated fabric collection for this easy-to-sew project.*

### materials

1⅛ yards of yellow print for pillowcase and blocks

⅓ yard of blue print for blocks and sashing

⅛ yard of light orange print for sashing

**Finished border:** 6×39¼"
**Finished block:** 6" square

## Cut the Fabrics

To make the best use of your fabrics, cut the pieces in the order that follows.

From yellow print, cut:
- 1—22×39¾" rectangle
- 1—8½×39¾" rectangle
- 16—2⅝" squares, cutting each in half diagonally for a total of 32 corner triangles

From blue print, cut:
- 8—3" squares for block centers
- 25—1¾×4" sashing strips

From light orange print, cut:
- 18—1¾" squares for sashing

## Assemble the Blocks

Referring to the Assemble the Blocks instructions on *page 24*, use one blue print 3" square and four yellow print triangles to make a block. Repeat to make a total of eight blocks.

## Assemble the Border

1. Lay out eight pieced blocks and nine blue print 1¾×4" sashing strips in a horizontal row, alternating them and beginning and ending the row with a sashing strip. Join the pieces to make a block row. The pieced block row should measure 4×39¾", including the seam allowances.

**2.** Lay out the nine orange print 1¾" sashing squares and eight blue print 1¾×4" sashing strips in a horizontal row, alternating them and beginning and ending the row with a sashing square. Join the pieces to make a sashing row. The pieced sashing row should measure 1¾×39¾", including the seam allowances. Repeat to make a second sashing row.

**3.** Referring to Diagram 3 for placement, lay out the sashing and block rows. Join the rows to make the pieced border. The pieced border should measure 6½×39¾", including the seam allowances.

## Assemble the Pillowcase

**1.** Referring to Diagram 3, lay out the pieced border and the two yellow print rectangles. Sew together the pieces to make a pillowcase unit.

**2.** With the right side inside, fold the pillowcase unit in half. Sew along the long raw edges. Then sew the unpieced end of the pillowcase unit closed; turn right side out. Press the seam allowances in one direction.

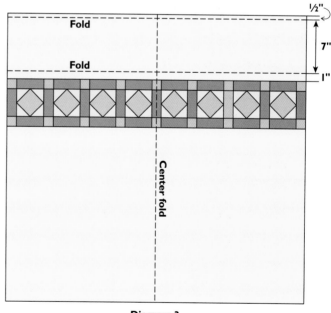

**Diagram 3**

**3.** Fold the unfinished edge under ½" and press. Fold the same edge under 7", leaving a 1"-wide strip along the outside edge of the pieced border. Topstitch the folded section in place to complete the pillowcase.

# two-COLOR TREASURES

*The idea of one simple quilt block sewn in just two colors dates back to the early 1800s. The two-color scheme may have developed from the desire to make a positive/negative repeat*

*pattern, much like the woven blankets of the day. Or, it might have stemmed from the desire to show off newly acquired wealth with the ability to purchase yard goods. Whatever their origin, two-color quilts remain classic to this day.*

# ROBBING
# PETER *to*
# PAY PAUL

*When pieced, the simple curved elements of this traditional pattern*

*result in a feeling of movement. Frequently stitched in just two colors,*

*this design takes off in a different direction when pieced with*

*a medley of fabrics. On the pages that follow you'll find additional*

*projects inspired by this enduring favorite: a plaid-and-stripe*

*floor pillow and a floral table runner.*

## *the* QUILT

### materials

4½ yards of muslin for blocks, borders, and binding

5½ yards of solid red for blocks

7½ yards of backing fabric

90×106" of quilt batting

**Finished quilt top: 83¾×99¼"**
**Finished block: 8¾" square**

Quantities specified for 44/45"-wide, 100% cotton fabrics. All measurements include a ¼" seam allowance unless otherwise stated.

### Cut the Fabrics

To make the best use of your fabrics, cut the pieces in the order that follows. The patterns are on *Pattern Sheet 2*. To make templates of the patterns, follow the instructions in Quilter's Schoolhouse, which begins on *page 146*.

From muslin, cut:
- 5—3×42" strips for side borders
- 4—2×42" strips for top and bottom borders
- 9—2½×42" binding strips
- 49 of Pattern A
- 200 of Pattern B

From solid red, cut:
- 50 of Pattern A
- 196 of Pattern B

*continued*

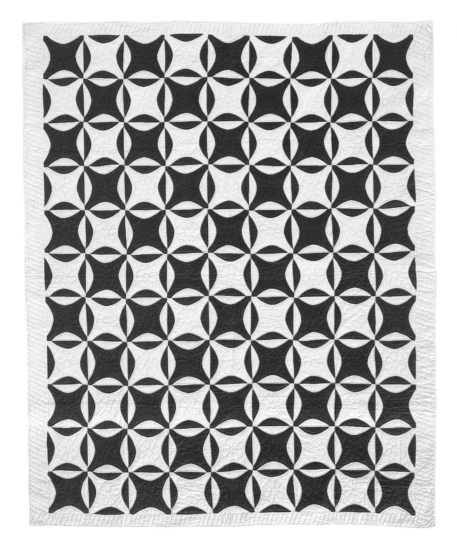

**2.** Sew together the pieces, removing each pin just before your needle reaches it. Press the seam allowances toward the red A piece. Add the remaining B pieces to the A piece in the same manner to make a Robbing Peter to Pay Paul block A (see Diagram 1). Pieced block A should measure 9¼" square, including the seam allowances.

**3.** Repeat steps 1 and 2 to make a total of 50 of block A. Then, referring to Diagram 2 for placement, use one muslin A piece and four solid red B pieces to make a block B. Repeat to make a total of 49 of block B.

## Assemble the Quilt Center

Referring to the photograph at *left,* lay out the blocks in 11 horizontal rows of nine blocks each, alternating blocks A and B. Sew together the blocks in each row. Press the seam allowances in one direction, alternating the direction with each row. Join the rows to make the quilt center. Press the seam allowances in one direction. The pieced quilt center should measure 79¼×96¾", including the seam allowances.

## Add the Borders

**1.** Cut and piece the muslin 3×42" strips to make the following:
  * 2—3×99¾" border strips
  Cut and piece the muslin 2×42" strips to make the following:
  * 2—2×79¼" border strips

**2.** Sew one short border strip to the top and bottom edges of the pieced quilt center. Then add one long border strip to each side edge of the pieced quilt center to complete the quilt top. Press all seam allowances toward the muslin border.

## Complete the Quilt

Layer the quilt top, batting, and backing according to the instructions in Quilter's Schoolhouse, which begins on *page 146.* Quilt as desired. This project was hand-quilted ¼" inside each piece. The Floral Medallion Quilting Design (see *Pattern Sheet 2*) was stitched in the center of each A piece and a 1"-wide diagonal grid was quilted in the borders. Use the muslin 2½×42" strips to bind the quilt according to the instructions in Quilter's Schoolhouse.

## Assemble the Robbing Peter to Pay Paul Blocks

**1.** With right sides together, place a muslin B piece atop a solid red A piece; match the center mark on the curved edge of the B piece with the center mark on one curved edge of the A piece. After pinning the center of the seam, pin each end; then pin generously in between. When pinning the curved seams, use slender pins and pick up only a few threads at each position.

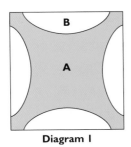

**Diagram 1**

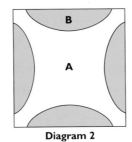

**Diagram 2**

*optional sizes*

If you'd like to make this quilt in a size other than for a double bed, use the information *below*.

| Alternate Quilt Sizes | Crib/Lap | Twin | King |
|---|---|---|---|
| **Number of blocks** | 24 (12 of each) | 54 (27 of each) | 144 (72 of each) |
| **Number of blocks wide by long** | 4×6 | 6×9 | 12×12 |
| **Border dimensions** | 2½" side | 2½" side | 2½" side |
| | 1½" top and bottom | 1½" top and bottom | 1½" top and bottom |
| **Finished Size** | 40×55½" | 57½×81¾" | 110×108" |
| **Yardage requirements** | | | |
| Muslin | 3 yards | 3½ yards | 10 yards |
| Solid red | 2½ yards | 3½ yards | 8½ yards |
| Backing | 2⅝ yards | 4⅞ yards | 9⅔ yards |
| Batting | 46×62" | 64×88" | 114×116" |

# *the* FLOOR PILLOW

*Plaid and stripe fabrics play a game of positive and negative when combined into the nine Robbing Peter to Pay Paul blocks used to compose this striking oversize pillow.*

## materials

¾ yard of black stripe for blocks

1⅓ yards of blue plaid for blocks and backing

½ yard of blue-and-black check for piping

3¼ yards of 1"-diameter cotton cording

26" square pillow form

**Finished pillow: 26¼" square**

## Cut the Fabrics

To make the best use of your fabrics, cut the pieces in the order that follows. This project uses "Robbing Peter to Pay Paul" patterns, which are on *Pattern Sheet 2*. To make templates of the patterns, follow the instructions in Quilter's Schoolhouse, which begins on *page 146*.

From black stripe, cut:
- 5 of Pattern A
- 16 of Pattern B

From blue plaid, cut:
- 4 of Pattern A
- 20 of Pattern B
- 1—26¾" square for backing

From blue-and-black check, cut:
- 1—18×42" rectangle, cutting and piecing it into enough 3⅝"-wide bias strips to total 110" in length (see Cutting Bias Strips in Quilter's Schoolhouse for specific instructions)

## Assemble the Blocks

Referring to the Assemble the Robbing Peter to Pay Paul Blocks instructions *opposite*, use one black stripe A piece and four blue plaid B pieces to make one block A. Repeat to make a total of five of block A. Then use one blue plaid A piece and four black stripe B pieces to make one block B. Repeat to make a total of four of block B.

## Assemble the Pillow

1. Lay out the blocks in three rows of three blocks each, alternating blocks A and B. Sew together the blocks in each row. Press the seam allowances toward block B. Join the rows to complete the pillow top. Press the seam allowances in one direction. The pieced pillow top should measure 26¾" square, including the seam allowances.

*continued*

**2.** With the wrong side inside, fold under 1½" at one end of the blue-and-black check bias strip. Fold the strip in half lengthwise with the wrong side inside. Insert the cording next to the folded edge, placing a cording end 1" from the folded end of the strip. Using a machine cording foot, sew through both fabric layers right next to the cording.

**3.** Starting on one side of the pieced pillow top, align the raw edges and stitch the covered cording to the right side of the pillow top. Begin stitching 1½" from the cording's folded end. Round the corners, making sure the corner curves match. As you stitch each corner, gently push the covered cording into place.

**4.** Once the cording is stitched around the edge of the pillow top, cut the end of the cording so that it will fit snugly into the folded opening at the beginning. The ends of the cording should abut inside the cording cover. Stitch the ends down and trim the raw edges as needed.

**5.** With wrong sides together, layer the pieced pillow top and pillow back. Stitch the layers together, leaving an opening for the pillow form along one edge. Turn pillow right side out. Insert the pillow form through the opening. Whipstitch the opening closed to complete the pillow.

# the TABLE RUNNER

*Let this sunny runner make your table company-ready. The curves of the Robbing Peter to Pay Paul blocks dictated the unusual shape of this tabletop quilt.*

## materials

½ yard of yellow print for blocks

½ yard of light yellow floral for blocks

¼ yard of yellow floral for binding

½ yard of backing fabric

18×36" of quilt batting

**Finished table runner top: 13¾×31¼"**

## Cut the Fabrics

To make the best use of your fabrics, cut the pieces in the order that follows. This project uses "Robbing Peter to Pay Paul" patterns, which are on *Pattern Sheet 2*. To make templates of the patterns, follow the instructions in Quilter's Schoolhouse, which begins on *page 146.*

From yellow print, cut:
*   2—3×14¼" rectangles
*   4—3×9¼" rectangles
*   4 of Pattern B
*   2 of Pattern A

From light yellow floral, cut:
*   1 of Pattern A
*   8 of Pattern B
*   2—3×9¼" rectangles

From yellow floral, cut:
*   1—9×30" rectangle, cutting and piecing it into enough 2½"-wide bias strips to total 90" in length

## Assemble the Blocks

Referring to the Assemble the Robbing Peter to Pay Paul Blocks instructions on *page 34,* use one yellow print A piece and four light yellow floral B pieces to make one block A. Repeat to make a second block. Then use one light yellow floral A piece and four yellow print B pieces to make one block B.

## Assemble the Table Runner Top

Referring to the photograph *above,* lay out the blocks, the four yellow print 3×9¼" rectangles, and the two light yellow floral 3×9¼" rectangles in three horizontal rows. Sew together the blocks and border rectangles in each row. Press the seam allowances in one direction, alternating the direction with each row. Join the rows. Press the seam allowances in one direction. Then sew one yellow print 3×14½" rectangle to each short edge to complete the table runner top. Press the seam allowances toward the border.

## Complete the Table Runner

Layer the table runner top, batting, and backing according to the instructions in Quilter's Schoolhouse, which begins on *page 146.*

Align the Border Cutting Template (see *Pattern Sheet 2*) with one corner of the table runner top. Trace around the template. Repeat tracing in the other three corners, reversing the pattern as needed to make the scalloped edge.

Quilt inside the traced lines as desired. This table runner was machine-quilted ¼" inside each piece; a floral medallion quilting design was quilted in the center of each A piece. Re-mark the scalloped edge as necessary. Trim the excess fabric and batting on the marked lines.

Use the yellow print 2½"-wide bias strips to bind the quilt according to the instructions in Quilter's Schoolhouse.

# STARS ABLAZE

*In the late 19th century, indigo blue and white surpassed all*

*other quilt color combinations in popularity. Today, more than 100*

*years later, this mix is as well-liked as ever by designer Jill Reber.*

*This quilt, which pairs two different quilt blocks, inspired a*

*likable trio of additional small projects.*

## *the* QUILT

### materials

3½ yards of muslin

3¾ yards of solid navy

4¼ yards of backing fabric

74" square of quilt batting

**Finished quilt top: 68" square**
**Finished blocks: 8" square**

Quantities specified for 44/45"-wide, 100% cotton fabrics. All measurements include a ¼" seam allowance unless otherwise stated.

### Cut the Fabrics

To make the best use of your fabrics, cut the pieces in the order that follows. There are no pattern pieces for this project. The letter designations are for placement only.

The border strips for this project are cut the length of the fabric (parallel to the selvage). These strip measurements are mathematically correct. You may wish to cut your border strips longer than specified to allow for sewing differences.

From muslin, cut:
- 2—2½×60½" inner border strips
- 2—2½×56½" inner border strips
- 100—2½" squares for block A, position D
- 25—5¼" squares, cutting each diagonally twice in an X for a total of 100 triangles for block A, position C
- 144—2⅞" squares, cutting each in half diagonally for a total of 288 triangles for block B, position B
- 24—4½" squares for block B, position A

From solid navy, cut:
- 2—4½×68½" outer border strips
- 2—4½×60½" outer border strips
- 148—2⅞" squares, cutting each in half diagonally for a total of 296 triangles for blocks A and B, position B
- 25—4½" squares for block A, position A
- 24—5¼" squares, cutting each diagonally twice in an X for a total of 96 triangles for block B, position C
- 7—2½×42" binding strips

*continued*

## Assemble Block A

1. Align the long edge of one solid navy B triangle with one short edge of a muslin C triangle; sew together.

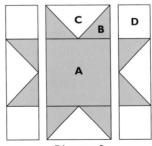

**Diagram 1**

Press open the attached solid navy B triangle. In the same manner, sew a second solid navy B triangle to the other short edge of the muslin C triangle; press open to make a Flying Geese unit (see Diagram 1). The pieced Flying Geese unit should measure 2½×4½", including the seam allowances. Repeat to make a total of four Flying Geese units.

2. Sew a Flying Geese unit to the top and bottom edges of a solid navy A square (see Diagram 2). Then add a muslin D square to each end of the remaining two Flying Geese units. Join one unit to each side edge of the solid navy A square to complete a block A (see Diagram 2). Pieced block A should measure 8½" square, including the seam allowances.

**Diagram 2**

3. Repeat steps 1 and 2 to make a total of 25 of block A.

## Assemble Block B

1. Align the long edge of one muslin B triangle with one short edge of a solid navy C triangle; sew together. Press open the attached muslin B triangle. In the same manner, sew a second muslin B triangle to the other short edge of the solid navy C triangle; press open to make a Flying Geese unit. The pieced Flying Geese unit should measure 2½×4½", including the seam allowances. Repeat to make a total of four Flying Geese units.

2. Sew together one muslin B triangle and one solid navy B triangle to make a triangle-square (see Diagram 3). Press the seam allowance toward the solid navy triangle. The pieced triangle-square should measure 2½" square, including the seam allowances. Repeat to make a total of four triangle-squares.

**Diagram 3**

3. Sew one Flying Geese unit to the top and bottom edges of a muslin A square (see Diagram 4). Then add a triangle-square to each end of the remaining two Flying Geese units. Join one unit to each side edge of the muslin A square to complete a block B (see Diagram 4). Pieced block B should measure 8½" square, including the seam allowances.

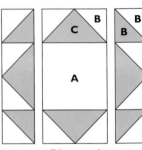

**Diagram 4**

4. Repeat steps 1 through 3 to make a total of 24 of block B.

## Assemble the Quilt Center

Referring to the photograph *above* for placement, lay out the pieced blocks in seven horizontal rows of seven blocks each, alternating blocks A and B.

Sew together the blocks in each row, pressing the seam allowances toward block A. Then join the rows to make the quilt center. Press the seam allowances in one direction. The pieced quilt center should measure 56½" square, including seam allowances.

## Add the Borders

1. Sew a muslin 2½×56½" inner border strip to the top and bottom edges of the pieced quilt center. Then add one muslin 2½×60½" inner border strip to each side edge of the pieced quilt center. Press all seam allowances toward the muslin borders.

Two-Color Treasures

**2.** Sew a solid navy 4½×60½" outer border strip to the top and bottom edges of the pieced quilt center. Then add one solid navy 4½×68½" outer border strip to each side edge of the pieced quilt center to complete the quilt top. Press all seam allowances toward the solid navy outer borders.

## Complete the Quilt

Layer the quilt top, batting, and backing according to the instructions in Quilter's Schoolhouse, which begins on *page 146*. Quilt as desired. Use the solid navy 2½×42" strips to bind the quilt according to the instructions in Quilter's Schoolhouse.

## Stars Ablaze Quilt
### *optional sizes*

If you'd like to make this quilt in a size other than a wall hanging, use the information *below*.

| Alternate Quilt Sizes | Crib | Twin | Full/Queen | King |
|---|---|---|---|---|
| Number of blocks | 20 | 54 | 108 | 144 |
| Number of blocks wide by long | 4×5 | 6×9 | 9×12 | 12×12 |
| Number of A blocks | 10 | 27 | 54 | 72 |
| Number of B blocks | 10 | 27 | 54 | 72 |
| Finished size | 44×52" | 60×84" | 84×108" | 108" square |
| | | | | |
| Yardage requirements | | | | |
| Muslin | 1⅝ yards | 3¾ yards | 6 yards | 7½ yards |
| Solid navy | 2¼ yards | 4 yards | 6 yards | 7¾ yards |
| Backing | 2¾ yards | 5 yards | 7½ yards | 9⅔ yards |
| Batting | 50×58" | 60×90" | 90×116" | 116" square |

## *the* TABLE RUNNER

*The secondary block in "Stars Ablaze," shown on page 38, gets top billing in this decorative table topper composed of three blocks framed by a wide border.*

### materials

¾ yard of blue floral for blocks, border, and binding

¼ yard of pink print for blocks and sashing

¼ yard of blue-and-white print for blocks

⅔ yard of backing fabric

23×41" of quilt batting

**Finished table runner top: 17×35"**

## Cut the Fabrics

To make the best use of your fabrics, cut the pieces in the order that follows.

From blue floral, cut:
- 3—4½" squares for block B, position A
- 6—2⅞" squares, cutting each in half diagonally for a total of 12 triangles for block B, position B
- 2—4×10½" border strips
- 2—4×35½" border strips
- 3—2½×42" binding strips

From pink print, cut:
- 3—5¼" squares, cutting each diagonally twice in an X for a total of 12 triangles for block B, position C
- 4—1½×8½" sashing strips
- 2—1½×28½" sashing strips

From blue-and-white print, cut:
- 18—2⅞" squares, cutting each in half diagonally for a total of 26 triangles for block B, position B

*continued*

floral 4×35½" border strip to each long edge of the table runner center to complete the table runner top. Press all seam allowances toward the blue floral border.

## Complete the Table Runner

Layer the table runner top, batting, and backing according to the instructions in Quilter's Schoolhouse, which begins on *page 146.* Quilt as desired. This table runner was machine-quilted in the ditch along the sashing and block seams. The center of each block was quilted with a medallion design. Use the blue floral 2½×42" strips to bind the quilt according to the instructions in Quilter's Schoolhouse.

# the '30s WALL QUILT

*Give "Stars Ablaze" a retro look with reproduction fabrics in vintage prints. Then set all of the blocks on point to further alter the quilt's look.*

## materials

2½ yards of muslin for blocks

20—⅛-yard pieces of assorted pastel prints for blocks

1 yard of solid green for blocks and binding

3 yards of backing fabric

53×63 of quilt batting

**Finished quilt top: 46½×57⅞"**

## Cut the Fabrics

To make the best use of your fabrics, cut the pieces in the order that follows.

**From muslin, cut:**

- 4—14" squares, cutting each diagonally twice in an X for a total of 16 side triangles (only 14 will be used)
- 72—2⅞" squares, cutting each in half diagonally for a total of 144 triangles for block B, position B

Two-Color Treasures

## Assemble the Blocks

Referring to the Assemble Block B instructions on *page 40,* use one blue floral A square, four pink print C triangles, four blue floral B triangles, and 12 blue-and-white print B triangles to make a block B. Repeat to make a total of three of block B.

## Assemble the Table Runner Center

Referring to the photograph *above,* lay out the three blocks and four pink print 1½×8½" sashing strips, alternating them.

Sew together the pieces to make a block row. Press the seam allowances toward the sashing strips. Then join one pink print 1½×28½" sashing strip to each long edge of the block row to make the table runner center. Press the seam allowances toward the sashing.

## Add the Border

Sew a blue floral 4×10½" border strip to each short edge of the table runner center. Then add a blue

- 80—2½" squares for block A, position D
- 20—5¼" squares, cutting each diagonally twice in an X for a total of 80 triangles for block A, position C
- 12—4½" squares for block B, position A
- 2—7¼" squares, cutting each in half diagonally for a total of 4 corner triangles

From *each* of the assorted pastel prints, cut:
- 1—4½" square for block A, position A
- 4—2⅞" squares, cutting each in half diagonally for a total of 8 triangles for block A, position B

From solid green, cut:
- 12—5¼" squares, cutting each diagonally twice in an X for a total of 48 triangles for block B, position C
- 24—2⅞" squares, cutting each in half diagonally for a total of 48 triangles for block B, position B
- 6—2½×42" binding strips

## Assemble the Blocks

1. Referring to the Assemble Block A instructions on *page 40*, use one assorted print A square, four muslin C triangles, eight assorted print B triangles, and four muslin D squares to make a block A. Repeat to make a total of 20 of block A.

2. Referring to the Assemble Block B instructions on *page 40*, use one muslin A square, 12 muslin B triangles, four solid green B triangles, and four solid green C triangles to make a block B. Repeat to make a total of 12 of block B.

## Assemble the Quilt Top

1. Referring to the photograph *below* for placement, lay out the blocks, alternating blocks A and B, and the 14 muslin side triangles in diagonal rows.

*continued*

**2.** Sew together the blocks in each diagonal row. Press the seam allowances in one direction, alternating the direction with each row. Then join the rows to make the quilt center. Add the muslin corner triangles to the pieced quilt center to complete the quilt top. Press the seam allowances in one direction. Trim the quilt top, leaving a ¾" border around the blocks, including the seam allowance.

## Complete the Quilt

Layer the quilt top, batting, and backing according to the instructions in Quilter's Schoolhouse, which begins on *page 146*. Quilt as desired. This quilt was machine-quilted with rows of diagonal stitching at 2" intervals. Use the solid green 2½×42" strips to bind the quilt according to the instructions in Quilter's Schoolhouse.

# *the* BATIK THROW

*Wonder how this project can be part of "Stars Ablaze"? It's the secondary block again, here pieced in nine assorted batiks. A tenth batik print borders the nine-block quilt top.*

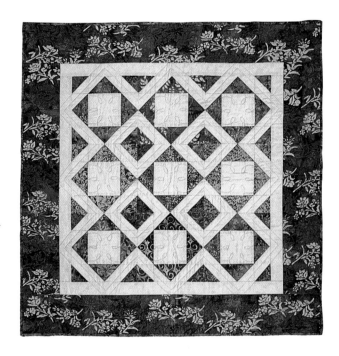

## materials

9—¼-yard pieces of assorted brown batiks for blocks

¾ yard of light tan print for blocks

⅝ yard of dark brown batik for border

⅓ yard of light brown batik for binding

1¼ yards of backing fabric

42" square of quilt batting

**Finished quilt top: 36" square**

## Cut the Fabrics

To make best use of your fabrics, cut the pieces in the order that follows.

From *each* of nine assorted brown batiks, cut:

- 1—5¼" square, cutting it diagonally twice in an X for a total of 4 triangles for block B, position C
- 2—2⅞" squares, cutting each in half diagonally for a total of 4 triangles for block B, position B

From light tan print, cut:

- 2—2×27½" inner border strips
- 2—2×24½" inner border strips
- 9—4½" squares for block B, position A
- 54—2⅞" squares, cutting each in half diagonally for a total of 108 triangles for block B, position B

From dark brown batik, cut:

- 2—5×27½" outer border strips
- 2—5×36½" outer border strips

From light brown batik cut:

- 4—2½×42" binding strips

## Assemble the Blocks

Referring to the Assemble Block B instructions on *page 40*, use one light tan print A square, 12 light tan print B triangles, four brown batik print B triangles, and four brown batik print C triangles to make a block B. Repeat to make a total of nine of block B.

## Assemble the Quilt Center

Referring to the photograph *opposite* for placement,
lay out the blocks in three rows of three blocks each.

Sew together the blocks in each row, pressing
the seam allowances in one direction, alternating
the direction with each row. Then join the rows to
make the quilt center. The pieced quilt center
should measure 24½" square, including the
seam allowances.

## Add the Borders

1. Sew a short inner border strip to the top and
bottom edges of the quilt center. Join one long
inner border strip to each side edge of the quilt
center. Press all seam allowances toward the
inner border.

2. Sew a short outer border strip to the top and
bottom edges of the quilt center. Join one long
outer border strip to each side edge of the quilt
center to complete the quilt top. Press all seam
allowances toward the outer border.

## Complete the Quilt

Layer the quilt top, batting, and backing according
to the instructions in Quilter's Schoolhouse, which
begins on *page 146*. Quilt as desired. The center
of each block was machine-quilted with the Looped
Medallion Quilting Design (see *Pattern Sheet 1*); the
outer part of each block was quilted in diagonal
rows. Use the light brown batik 2½×42" strips to
bind the quilt according to the instructions in
Quilter's Schoolhouse.

# TOYLAND

*Redwork, a form of embroidery that uses red thread to trace simple line drawings, was all the rage from the late 1880s through the 1930s. It has developed a new following in recent years. Designer Cindy Taylor Oates used the technique to produce this lively quilt and pillow. These adaptable blocks and borders are sewn into a number of projects in the pages that follow.*

## the QUILT

### materials

2¾ yards of white print for blocks and borders

¾ yard of red large polka dot for blocks, borders, and binding

¾ yard of red small polka dot for blocks, borders, and binding

9—¼-yard pieces of assorted red prints for blocks and borders

3 yards of backing fabric

52×64" of quilt batting

Red embroidery floss

Red fine-tip permanent Pigma pen

**Finished quilt top: 46×58"**
**Finished blocks: 6" square**

Quantities specified for 44/45"-wide, 100% cotton fabrics. All measurements include a ¼" seam allowance unless otherwise stated.

## Cut the Fabrics

To make the best use of your fabrics, cut the pieces in the order that follows. Cut the border strips the length of the fabric (parallel to the selvage). The strip measurements are mathematically correct. You may wish to cut your border strips longer than specified to allow for possible sewing differences.

From white print, cut:
- 1—20×42" rectangle for embroidery foundation
- 2—2½×46½" middle border strips
- 2—2½×38½" middle border strips
- 24—2½×6½" rectangles
- 62—2½" squares
- 15—2½×17" strips
- 42—2⅞" squares

From red large polka dot, cut:
- 3—2½×42" binding strips
- 48—2½" squares
- 4—2⅞" squares

From red small polka dot, cut:
- 3—2½×42" binding strips
- 48—2½" squares
- 6—2⅞" squares

From nine assorted red prints, cut:
- 12—2½×17" strips
- 32—2⅞" squares
- 50—2½" squares

*continued*

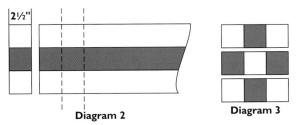

**Diagram 2**       **Diagram 3**

3. Sew together one strip set A segment and two strip set B segments to make a Nine-Patch block (see Diagram 3). Press the seam allowances toward the center segment. The Nine-Patch block should measure 6½" square, including the seam allowances. Repeat to make a total of 18 Nine-Patch blocks.

## Embroider the Squares

1. Starting in the upper left corner of the white print 20×42" embroidery foundation rectangle, about 1" from the edges, use a quilting pencil to lightly mark 17 adjoining 6½" squares. Do not cut the squares apart.

2. Center and trace one of the nine "Toyland" embroidery designs, found on *pages 57–59*, onto each square using a fine-tip red permanent Pigma pen. Project designer Cindy Taylor Oates traced eight of the designs twice and one design once.

3. Using a stem stitch and two strands of red embroidery floss, embroider the designs. Cindy uses an embroidery hoop when stitching to keep the fabric taut.

   To stem-stitch pull the needle up at A. Insert the needle back into the fabric at B, about ⅜" away from A. Holding the thread out of the way, bring the needle back up at C and pull the thread through so it lies flat against the fabric. The distances between points A, B, and C should be equal. Pull with equal tautness after each stitch.

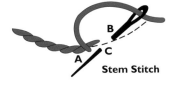

**Stem Stitch**

4. When you've completed the embroidery, cut the squares apart on the drawn lines.

## Assemble the Snowball Blocks

1. For accurate sewing lines, use a quilting pencil to mark a diagonal line on the wrong side of 34 of the red small polka dot 2½" squares and 34 of the

## Assemble the Nine-Patch Blocks

1. Aligning long edges, sew two red print 2½×17" strips to a white print 2½×17" strip to make a strip set A (see Diagram 1). Press the seam allowances toward the red print strips. Repeat to make a total of three of strip set A. Cut the strip sets into 2½"-wide segments for a total of 18.

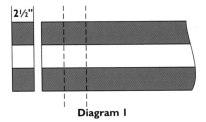

**Diagram 1**

2. Aligning long edges, sew two white print 2½×17" strips to a red print 2½×17" strip to make a strip set B (see Diagram 2). Press the seam allowances toward the red print strip. Repeat to make a total of six of strip set B. Cut the strip sets into 2½"-wide segments for a total of 36.

red large polka dot 2½" squares. (To prevent your fabric from stretching as you draw the lines, place 220-grit sandpaper under the squares.)

2. With right sides together, align one red small polka dot square with one corner of an embroidered square (see Diagram 4; note the placement of the sewing line). Stitch on the sewing line. Trim the seam allowance to ¼". Press open the attached red polka dot triangle.

**Diagram 4**

3. As in Step 2, sew a second red small polka dot square to the opposite corner of the embroidered square; trim and press open.

4. Repeat with two red large polka dot squares and the remaining two corners of the embroidered square; trim and press to make a Snowball block. The pieced Snowball block should measure 6½" square, including the seam allowances.

5. Repeat steps 2 through 4 to make a total of 17 Snowball blocks.

## Assemble the Quilt Center

Referring to the photograph *opposite,* lay out the 18 Nine-Patch blocks and the 17 Snowball blocks in seven horizontal rows, alternating the blocks. Sew together the blocks in each row. Press the seam allowances toward the Snowball blocks. Then join the rows to make the quilt center. Press the seam allowances in one direction. The pieced quilt center should measure 30½×42½", including seam allowances.

## Assemble and Add the Inner Border

1. For accurate sewing lines, use a quilting pencil to mark a diagonal line on the wrong side of 14 of the red small polka dot 2½" squares and 14 of the red large polka dot 2½" squares.

2. With raw edges aligned, place a marked red small polka dot square on the left end of a white print 2½×6½" rectangle (see Diagram 5; note the placement of the sewing line). Stitch on the marked sewing line. Trim the seam to ¼". Press open the

attached red small polka dot triangle. Stitch a marked red large polka dot square to the opposite end of the rectangle in the same manner; trim and press to make a rectangle unit. Repeat to make a total of six rectangle units.

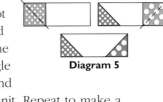

**Diagram 5**

3. Lay out three rectangle units and two white print 2½×6½" rectangles in a horizontal row, beginning and ending with a rectangle unit. Sew together the rectangles to make the top inner border strip. Press the seam allowances toward the white print rectangles. The pieced top inner border strip should measure 2½×30½", including the seam allowances. Sew the pieced inner border strip to the top edge of the pieced quilt center.

4. Repeat Step 3 to make the bottom inner border strip; sew to the bottom edge of the pieced quilt center.

5. With raw edges aligned, place a marked red large polka dot square on the left end of a white print 2½×6½" rectangle. Stitch on the marked sewing line; trim and press. Sew a marked red small polka dot square to the opposite end of the rectangle in the same manner; trim and press to make a rectangle unit. Repeat to make a total of eight rectangle units.

6. Lay out four rectangle units, three white print 2½×6½" rectangles, and two white print 2½" squares in a vertical row, beginning and ending with a white print 2½" square. Join the pieces to make a side inner border strip. Press the seam allowances toward the white print pieces. The pieced side inner border strip should measure 2½×46½", including the seam allowances. Sew to one side edge of the pieced quilt top.

7. Repeat Step 6 for a second side inner border strip; sew to the remaining side edge of the pieced quilt center.

## Add the Middle Border

1. Sew a white print 2½×46½" middle border strip to each side edge of the pieced quilt center. Press seam allowances toward the white print middle border.

*continued*

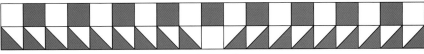

**2.** Sew one white print 2½×38½" middle border strip to the top and bottom edges of the pieced quilt center. Press the seam allowances toward the white print middle border.

**Diagram 7**

## Add the Outer Border

**1.** For accurate sewing lines, use a quilting pencil to mark a diagonal line on the wrong side of the six red small polka dot 2⅞" squares, the four red large polka dot 2⅞" squares, and the 32 assorted red print 2⅞" squares.

**2.** With right sides together, join each marked red print and polka dot square to a white print 2⅞" square, sewing ¼" on each side of the marked line (see Diagram 6). Cut apart on the marked lines to make 84 triangle-squares. Press the seam allowances toward the red print triangles. Each pieced triangle-square should measure 2½" square, including the seam allowances.

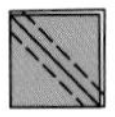

**Diagram 6**

**3.** Referring to Diagram 7, lay out 18 triangle-squares, 11 white print 2½" squares, and nine red print 2½" squares in two rows; note the placement of the triangle-squares.

**4.** Sew together the squares in each row. Then join the rows to make the top outer border strip. The pieced top outer border strip should measure 4½×38½", including the seam allowances. Join the top outer border strip to the top edge of the pieced quilt center.

**5.** Repeat steps 3 and 4 to make the bottom outer border strip; join to the bottom edge of the pieced quilt center.

**6.** Referring to Diagram 8, lay out 24 triangle-squares, 18 white print 2½" squares, and 16 red print 2½" squares in two rows; note the placement of the triangle-squares.

**7.** Sew together the squares in each row. Then join the rows to make the side outer border strip. The pieced side outer border strip should measure 4½×58½", including the seam allowances. Join the side outer border strip to one side edge of the pieced quilt center.

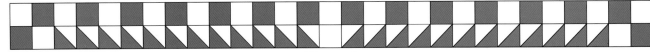

**Diagram 8**

## Toyland Quilt
*optional sizes*

If you'd like to make this quilt in a size other than given, use the information *below*.

| Alternate Quilt Sizes | Twin | Full/Queen | King |
|---|---|---|---|
| **Number of blocks** | 39 Nine-Patch | 72 Nine-Patch | 113 Nine-Patch |
| | 38 Snowball | 71 Snowball | 112 Snowball |
| **Number of blocks wide by long** | 7×11 | 11×13 | 15 square |
| **Finished size** | 58×82" | 82×94" | 106" square |
| | | | |
| **Yardage requirements** | | | |
| White print - pieced borders | 4⅝ yards | 6¾ yards | 10½ yards |
| Large polka dot | 1⅓ yards | 2⅓ yards | 3 yards |
| Small polka dot | 1⅓ yards | 2⅓ yards | 3 yards |
| Assorted red prints | ¼ yard each of nine | ⅓ yard each of nine | ⅓ yard each of nine |
| Backing | 3⅝ yards | 7⅓ yards | 9⅓ yards |
| Batting | 64×88" | 88×100" | 112" square |
| Binding | ½ yard | ⅝ yard | ⅞ yard |

**8.** Repeat steps 6 and 7 to make a second side outer border strip; join to the remaining side edge of the pieced quilt center to complete the quilt top.

## Complete the Quilt

Layer the quilt top, batting, and backing according to the instructions in Quilter's Schoolhouse, which begins on *page 146*. Quilt as desired. This quilt was machine-quilted diagonally through the Nine-Patch blocks and into the borders. Use the red large polka dot and red small polka dot 2½×42" strips to bind the quilt according to the instructions in Quilter's Schoolhouse.

A blue star fabric and assorted pastels combine for another version of "Toyland." For a girl's room try substituting a pink floral for the blue fabric.

# *the* PILLOWCASE

*As a companion to the quilt, a standard-size pillowcase features three "Toyland" embroidery designs stitched on one block.*

## Materials for Pillow

¼ yard of white print

⅛ yard of red plaid

¾ yard of red large polka dot

¼ yard of red small polka dot

⅛ yard of red stripe

½ yard of red large check

24×30" of muslin

24×30" of thin quilt batting

Red embroidery floss

1 package of red jumbo rickrack

Red fine-tip permanent Pigma pen

9—¾"-diameter red buttons

**Finished pillowcase: fits a standard 20×26" or 20×28" pillow**

## Cut the Fabrics

To make the best use of your fabrics, cut the pieces in the order that follows.

From white print, cut:
• 1—14½×8½" rectangle for embroidery foundation
• 2—2×21" strips

From red plaid, cut:
• 2—1½×16½" strips
• 2—1½×8½" strips

*continued*

From red large polka dot, cut:
- 2—5¾×16½" strips
- 2—16½×21" rectangles
- 2—2½" squares

From red small polka dot, cut:
- 2—4¼×21" strips
- 2—2½" squares

From red stripe, cut:
- 2—1½×21" strips

From red large check, cut:
- 1—18" square, cutting it into enough 2½"-wide bias strips to total 100" in length (see Cutting Bias Strips in Quilter's Schoolhouse, which begins on *page 146* for specific instructions)

From red jumbo rickrack, cut:
- 4—23"-long pieces

## Stitch the Embroidered Block

1. Trace three of the "Toyland" embroidery designs, found on *pages 57–59*, onto the white print 14½×8½" rectangle using a fine-tip red permanent Pigma pen. No design should be closer to an edge than 1".

2. Using a stem stitch and two strands of red embroidery floss, embroider the designs.

3. For accurate sewing lines, use a quilting pencil to mark a diagonal line on the wrong side of the two red small polka dot 2½" squares and the two red large polka dot 2½" squares.

4. Referring to Assemble the Snowball Blocks, steps 2 through 4, on *page 49*, use the embroidered rectangle and four marked squares to make a Snowball block.

5. Sew one red plaid 1½×8½" strip to each side edge of the embroidered rectangle. Then add one red plaid 1½×16½" strip to the top and bottom edges of the embroidered rectangle to complete the center rectangle. Press all seam allowances toward the red plaid strips.

## Add the Borders

1. Sew one red large polka dot 5¾×16½" strip to the top and bottom edges of the center rectangle. Press the seam allowances toward the red large polka dot strips.

2. Sew one red stripe 1½×21" strip to each side edge of the center rectangle. Press the seam allowances toward the red stripe strips.

3. Baste a 23"-long piece of red jumbo rickrack to the right side of each long edge of a white print 2×21" strip. The rickrack should be centered on the ¼" seam allowances. (Designer Cindy Taylor Oates started the rickrack at the same point in the wave on each side of the strip.) Repeat on he second white print 2×21" strip.

4. Sew one white print strip to each side edge of the center rectangle. Press the seams toward the red stripe strips.

5. Sew one red small polka dot 4¼×21" strip to each side edge of the center rectangle to complete the pieced pillowcase top. Press the seam allowances toward the red small polka dot strips.

## Quilt the Pillowcase Top

Layer the pillowcase top, batting, and muslin according to the instructions in Quilter's Schoolhouse, which begins on *page 146.* Quilt as desired. Baste through all layers ¼" from the raw edges. Trim the batting and muslin even with the quilted pillowcase top. Using a small plate as a template, curve the corners of the quilted pillowcase top. Baste the corners ¼" from the raw edges. Sew three buttons to each white strip.

## Complete the Pillowcase

1. Turn under 1" on one long edge of each red large polka dot 16½×21" rectangle; press. Turn under again 1"; press. Machine-stitch through all layers close to the second folded edge using red thread.

2. Stitch three buttonholes centered vertically in the hemmed edge of one of the rectangles. Stitch three buttons on the remaining rectangle, centering them on the hemmed edge and making sure they correspond to the buttonholes. Button the hemmed rectangles together to make the pillowcase back.

3. With wrong sides together, pin the pillowcase top to the pillowcase back. Using the red large check 2½"-wide bias strips, bind the pillowcase top to the pillowcase back according to the instructions in Quilter's Schoolhouse.

# the
# ANIMAL
# WALL QUILT

*In another twist on the "Toyland" quilt, the motifs in this wall hanging are colored with crayons instead of embroidered. Ask your favorite child to lend a hand with this project.*

**Finished quilt top: 20" square**

## Cut the Fabrics

To make the best use of your fabrics, cut the pieces in the order that follows.

*continued*

## materials

¼ yard of cream print for blocks

¼ yard *each* of peach polka dot, brown polka dot, gold plaid, and green plaid for blocks

¼ yard of tan print for blocks

¼ yard of solid brown for binding

¾ yard of backing fabric

26" square of quilt batting

Water-erasable pen

Crayons

Black embroidery floss

From cream print, cut:
- 4—6½" squares

From *each* of the peach polka dot, brown polka dot, gold plaid, and green plaid, cut:
- 3—2⅞" squares
- 13—2½" squares for blocks

From tan print, cut:
- 12—2⅞" squares
- 4—2½" squares

From solid brown, cut:
- 3—2½×42" binding strips

## Color and Embroider the Squares

1. Trace one of the "Toyland" embroidery designs, found on *pages 57–59*, onto each cream print 6½" square with a water-erasable pen.

2. Referring to the photograph on *page 53* for color options, color the designs with crayons.

3. To set the crayons, place a colored design face down on an ironing board. (You'll want to protect your surface with something that can be discarded.) With your iron on a warm heat setting, press each block, being careful not to scorch your designs. Set all four designs in the same manner.

4. Using two strands of black embroidery floss, stem-stitch around each colored design.

## Assemble the Blocks

Referring to the Assemble the Snowball Blocks instructions, which begin on *page 48,* use one embroidered square and four peach polka dot 2½" squares to make a Snowball block. Repeat with the remaining embroidered squares and four brown polka dot 2½" squares, four gold plaid 2½" squares, and four green plaid 2½" squares.

## Assemble the Quilt Center

Sew together the four Snowball blocks in two rows of two blocks each. Press the seam allowances in opposite directions. Then join the rows to complete the quilt center. Press the seam allowances in one direction. The pieced quilt center should measure 12½" square, including the seam allowances.

## Assemble and Add the Border

1. Referring to the Add the Outer Border instructions, steps 1 and 2, on *page 50,* use 12 tan print 2⅞" squares, three peach polka dot 2⅞" squares, three brown polka dot 2⅞" squares, three gold plaid

2⅞" squares, and three green plaid 2⅞" squares to make a total of 24 triangle-squares.

2. Referring to the photograph on *page 53,* lay out three peach polka dot triangle-squares, three gold plaid triangle-squares, and six assorted peach polka dot, brown polka dot, gold plaid, and green plaid 2½" squares in two rows; note the placement of the triangle-squares.

3. Sew together the squares in each row. Press the seam allowances in opposite directions. Then join the rows to make a top outer border strip. The pieced top outer border strip should measure 4½×12½", including the seam allowances. Join the top outer border strip to the top edge of the pieced quilt center.

4. Repeat steps 2 and 3 to make a bottom outer border strip using three green plaid triangle-squares and three brown polka dot triangle-squares; join to the bottom edge of the pieced quilt center.

5. Referring to the photograph on *page 53,* lay out three peach polka dot triangle-squares, three green plaid triangle-squares, two tan print 2½" squares, and 12 assorted peach polka dot, brown polka dot, gold plaid, and green plaid 2½" squares.

6. Sew together the squares in each row. Press the seam allowances in opposite directions. Then join the rows to make a side outer border strip. The pieced side outer border strip should measure 4½×20½", including the seam allowances. Join the side outer border strip to one side edge of the pieced quilt center.

7. Repeat steps 5 and 6 to make a second side outer border strip using three gold plaid triangle-squares and three brown polka dot triangle-squares; join to the remaining side edge of the pieced quilt center to complete the quilt top.

## Complete the Quilt

Layer the quilt top, batting, and backing according to the instructions in Quilter's Schoolhouse, which begins on *page 146.* Quilt as desired. This wall hanging was machine-quilted following the seam lines and the embroidery lines; outer borders were quilted about ¼" from seam lines. Use the solid brown 2½×42" strips to bind the quilt according to the instructions in Quilter's Schoolhouse.

# the TRADITIONAL THROW

*Take away the embroidery blocks from the "Toyland" quilt and you'll uncover a Nine-Patch block. Piece this block in traditional prints for a classic throw or wall quilt.*

**Finished quilt top: 42" square**
**Finished block: 10" square**

*continued*

## materials

5—⅛-yard pieces of assorted dark red prints for blocks

9—⅛-yard pieces of assorted light prints for blocks

4—⅛-yard pieces of assorted dark green prints for blocks

⅝ yard of light red print for blocks

5—⅛-yard pieces of assorted dark blue prints for blocks

⅜ yard of green check for blocks

¾ yard of solid dark blue for sashing and binding

⅝ yard of dark red floral for border

1⅓ yards of backing fabric

48" square of quilt batting

## Cut the Fabrics

To make the best use of your fabrics, cut the pieces in the order that follows.

From *each* of five assorted dark red prints, cut:
- 5—2½" squares

From *each* of four assorted dark red prints, cut:
- 8—2½" squares

From *each* of nine assorted light prints, cut:
- 4—2½" squares

From *each* of four assorted dark green prints, cut:
- 5—2½" squares

From light red print, cut:
- 20—2½×6½" rectangles
- 20—2½" squares
- 16—1½" squares for sashing

From *each* of five assorted dark blue prints, cut:
- 8—2½" squares

From green check, cut:
- 16—2½×6½" rectangles
- 16—2½" squares

From solid dark blue, cut:
- 24—1½×10½" sashing strips
- 5—2½×42" binding strips

From dark red floral, cut:
- 2—4½×42½" border strips
- 2—4½×34½" border strips

## Assemble the Nine-Patch Blocks

1. Referring to Diagram 3 on *page 48*, lay out four light print 2½" squares and five dark red print 2½" squares in three horizontal rows. Sew together the squares in each row. Press the seam allowances toward the dark red print squares. Then join the rows to make a dark red Nine-Patch block. Repeat to make a total of five dark red Nine-Patch blocks.

2. Repeat Step 1 using four light print 2½" squares and five dark green print 2½" squares to make a dark green Nine-Patch block. Repeat to make a total of four dark green Nine-Patch blocks.

## Assemble the Block Border

1. Referring to the Assemble and Add the Inner Border instructions, steps 1 and 2, on *page 49*, use the 40 dark blue print 2½" squares and the 20 light red print 2½×6½" rectangles to make 20 rectangle units.

2. Sew one rectangle unit to the side edges of each dark red Nine-Patch block.

3. Join one light red print 2½" square to each end of the 10 remaining rectangle units. Sew one pieced rectangle unit to the top and bottom edges of the dark red Nine-Patch blocks.

4. Repeat steps 1 through 3 above using the 16 green check 2½×6½" rectangles, the 32 dark red print 2½" squares, the 16 green check 2½" squares, and the four dark green Nine-Patch blocks.

## Add the Sashing

1. Referring to the photograph on *page 55*, lay out the nine Nine-Patch blocks, the 24 solid dark blue 1½×10½" sashing strips, and the 16 light red print 1½" sashing squares in seven horizontal rows.

2. Sew together the pieces in each row. Press the seam allowances toward the solid dark blue sashing strips. Then join the rows to complete the quilt center. Press the seam allowances in one direction. The pieced quilt center should measure 34½" square, including the seam allowances.

## Add the Border

Sew a dark red floral print 4½×34½" border strip to each side edge of the pieced quilt center. Then add a dark red floral print 4½×42½" border strip to the top and bottom edges of the pieced quilt center to complete the quilt top. Press all seam allowances toward the red floral border.

## Complete the Quilt

Layer the quilt top, batting, and backing according to the instructions in Quilter's Schoolhouse, which begins on *page 146*. Quilt as desired. The blocks in this wall hanging were machine-quilted in the ditch and in a X through the center; the borders were quilted using straight lines. Use the solid dark blue 2½×42" strips to bind the quilt according to the instructions in Quilter's Schoolhouse.

*patterns*

patterns

Two-Color Treasures

# *the* LOG CABIN COLLECTION

The versatile Log Cabin block, long the symbol

of the American frontier, dates back to the 1860s.

The fabric strips in this block represent the

interlocking logs of a pioneer cabin, laid row

upon row. A red block in

the middle symbolizes the

hearth as the center of the

cabin, while a gold or

yellow center represents a candle

lighting the cabin window.

# CHRISTMAS *by* CANDLELIGHT

*Welcome the holiday with plenty of country charm. Jean Lepper composed this seasonal wall hanging with traditional Log Cabin blocks and simple appliqué. On the pages that follow you'll find a trio of additional Log Cabin-inspired projects—for holiday, birthday, or any day.*

## *the* QUILT

**Finished quilt top: 43" square**
**Finished block: 11" square**

Quantities specified for 44/45"-wide, 100% cotton fabrics. All measurements include a ¼" seam allowance unless otherwise stated.

### Cut the Fabrics

To make the best use of your fabrics, cut the pieces in the order that follows. The measurements for the border strips are mathematically correct. You may wish to cut your border strips longer than specified to allow for possible sewing differences. In the diagrams, the letter designations are for placement only.

The patterns for this project (X, Y, and Z) are on *Pattern Sheet 2*. To use fusing-adhesive material for appliqué, as was done on this project, complete the following steps.

*continued*

## materials

¾ yard total of assorted dark red and dark green prints for Log Cabin blocks

¾ yard total of assorted light gold prints for Log Cabin blocks

1¼ yards of gold-and-red plaid for outer border and binding

⅜ yard of cream print for candle blocks and corner blocks

⅓ yard of dark green print for Log Cabin blocks, corner blocks, and inner border

⅛ yard of red print for candle blocks and corner blocks

⅛ yard of green check for candle blocks

1 skein each of gold, green, and black embroidery floss

⅓ yard of fusing-adhesive material

1½ yards of backing fabric

48" square of quilt batting

1. Lay the fusing-adhesive material, paper side up, over pattern pieces X, Y, and Z. With a pencil, trace each piece the number of times indicated, leaving ½" between tracings. Cut out, cutting about ¼" outside of the traced lines.

2. Following the manufacturer's instructions, press the fusing-adhesive pieces onto the backs of the designated fabrics. Let the fabrics cool, then cut out the pattern pieces on the drawn lines. Peel off the paper from the fabric backs.

**From assorted dark red and dark green prints, randomly cut:**
- 4—1½×2½" B rectangles
- 4—1½×3½" C rectangles
- 4—1½×4½" D rectangles
- 9—1½×5½" E rectangles
- 9—1½×6½" F rectangles
- 9—1½×7½" G rectangles
- 9—1½×8½" H rectangles
- 9—1½×9½" I rectangles
- 9—1½×10½" J rectangles
- 4—1½×11½" K rectangles

**From assorted light gold prints, cut:**
- 4—1½" A squares
- 4—1½×2½" B rectangles
- 4—1½×3½" C rectangles
- 4—1½×4½" D rectangles
- 4—1½×5½" E rectangles
- 9—1½×6½" F rectangles
- 9—1½×7½" G rectangles
- 9—1½×8½" H rectangles
- 9—1½×9½" I rectangles
- 9—1½×10½" J rectangles
- 5—1½×11½" K rectangles
- 5 of Pattern X

**From gold-and-red plaid, cut:**
- 4—4½×33½" outer border strips
- 1—18×42" rectangle, cutting it into enough 2"-wide bias strips to total 180" in length (see Quilter's Schoolhouse, which begins on *page 146,* for specific cutting instructions)

**From cream print, cut:**
- 10—1½×5½" E rectangles
- 10—1½×2½" B rectangles
- 5—2½×3½" L rectangles
- 5—1⅞" squares, cutting each in half diagonally for a total of 10 M triangles
- 4—5½" squares

**From dark green print, cut:**
- 4—1½×33½" inner border strips
- 4—1½" A squares
- 12 of Pattern Y

**From red print, cut:**
- 5—1½×2½" B rectangles
- 8 of Pattern Z

**From green check, cut:**
- 5—1⅞" squares, cutting each in half diagonally for a total of 10 M triangles
- 5—1½" A squares

## Assemble the Log Cabin Blocks

1. Referring to Diagram 1, join a light gold print A square to a dark green print A square. Press the seam allowance toward the light gold print square.

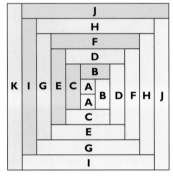

**Diagram 1**

2. Working counterclockwise around the pieced A squares, add rectangles in alphabetical order as shown in Diagram 1. Begin with a light gold B rectangle on the right-hand side of the A squares. Then join a red or green B rectangle, a red or green C rectangle, and so on until you've completed the block. As you add each piece, press the seam allowance toward the outside of the block. The pieced Log Cabin block should measure 11½" square, including the seam allowances.

3. Repeat steps 1 and 2 to make a total of four Log Cabin blocks.

## Assemble the Candle Blocks

1. Referring to Diagram 2, sew together one green check M triangle and one cream print M triangle to make a triangle-square. Press the seam allowance toward the green triangle. Repeat to make a second green-and-cream triangle-square.

**Diagram 2**

**2.** Join a triangle-square to opposite sides of a green check A square to make a candleholder unit (see Diagram 3). Press the seam allowances toward the A square.

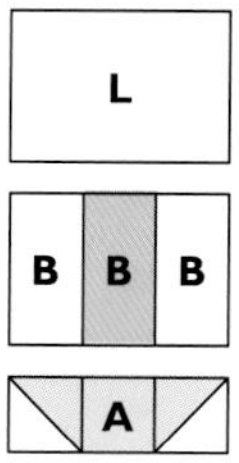

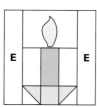

**Diagram 3**

**3.** Sew a cream print B rectangle to opposite sides of a red print B rectangle to make a candlestick unit.

**4.** Sew a cream print L rectangle to the top edge of the candlestick unit. Then join the candleholder unit to the lower edge to make a candle unit. Referring to Diagram 4, add a cream print E rectangle to each side of the candle unit.

**5.** Fuse the gold print X candle flame to the cream print rectangle in the candle unit (see Diagram 4). Using two strands of gold embroidery floss, blanket-stitch the flame in place. (For specific information on blanket stitching, see Quilter's Schoolhouse, which begins on *page 146.*)

**Diagram 4**

**6.** Working clockwise around the candle unit, add rectangles in alphabetical order as shown in Diagram 5. Begin with a red or green E rectangle on the right-hand side of a candle unit. Then join a red or green F rectangle, a gold F rectangle, and so on until you've completed the candle block. As you add each piece, press the seam allowance toward the outside of the block. The pieced candle block should measure 11½" square, including the seam allowances.

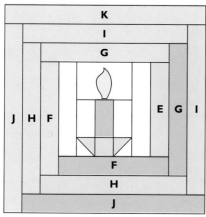

**Diagram 5**

**7.** Repeat steps 1 through 6 to make a total of five candle blocks.

## Assemble the Quilt Center

Referring to the photograph on *page 62,* lay out the Log Cabin and candle blocks in three rows. Sew together the blocks in each row. Press the seam allowances toward the candle blocks. Then join the rows to complete the quilt center. The pieced quilt center should measure 33½" square, including the seam allowances.

## Add the Borders

**1.** Position and fuse three dark green print Y holly leaves and two red print Z holly berries to a cream print 5½" square to make a corner block (refer to the photograph on *page 62* for placement). Using two strands of green embroidery floss, blanket-stitch the appliqué leaves in place. Using two strands of black floss, blanket-stitch the appliqué berries in place. Repeat to make a total of four corner blocks.

**2.** Sew together one dark green print 1½×33½" inner border strip and one red-and-gold plaid 4½×33½" outer border strip to make a border strip set. Press the seam allowance toward the plaid strip. Repeat to make a total of four border strip sets. Sew one border strip set to the top and bottom edges of the pieced quilt center. Press the seam allowances toward the border.

**3.** Stitch one appliquéd corner block to each end of the remaining border strip sets. Stitch one pieced border strip set to each side edge of the pieced quilt center to complete the quilt top. Press the seam allowances toward the border.

## Complete the Quilt

Layer the quilt top, batting, and backing according to the instructions in Quilter's Schoolhouse, which begins on *page 146.* Quilt as desired. The candle block backgrounds and outer border were hand-quilted in a diagonal grid; the strips in the Log Cabin blocks were hand-quilted down the middle. Use the gold-and-red plaid 2"-wide bias strips to bind the quilt according to the instructions in Quilter's Schoolhouse.

*continued*

## Christmas by Candlelight Quilt
## *optional sizes*

If you'd like to make this quilt in a size other than for a wall hanging, check the information *below*.

| Alternate Quilt Sizes | Crib/Lap | Twin | Double/Queen | King |
|---|---|---|---|---|
| **Number of blocks** | 6 Log Cabin/6 candle | 21 Log Cabin/21 candle | 28 Log Cabin/28 candle | 36 Log Cabin/36 candle |
| **Number of blocks wide by long** | 3×4 | 6×7 | 7×8 | 8×9 |
| **Finished size** | 43×54" | 76×87" | 87×98" | 98×109" |
| | | | | |
| **Yardage requirements** | | | | |
| Assorted dark red and green prints for blocks | 1¼ yards | 3½ yards | 5¼ yards | 6⅝ yards |
| Assorted light gold prints for blocks | 1¼ yards | 3½ yards | 5¼ yards | 6⅝ yards |
| Gold-and-red plaid for outer border and binding | 1¼ yards | 1¾ yards | 2 yards | 2¼ yards |
| Cream print for blocks | ⅜ yard | ¾ yard | 1 yards | 1½ yards |
| Dark green print for blocks and inner border | ⅓ yard | ½ yard | ½ yard | ⅝ yard |
| Red print for blocks | ⅛ yard | ¼ yard | ¼ yard | ⅜ yard |
| Green check for blocks | ⅛ yard | ¼ yard | ¼ yard | ⅜ yard |
| Backing | 2¾ yards | 5¼ yards | 7¾ yards | 8⅔ yards |
| Batting | 49×60" | 82×93" | 93×104" | 104×115" |

## *the* BIRTHDAY WALL HANGING

*We paired celebratory candle blocks from "Christmas by Candlelight" with small Log Cabin blocks for a cheerful banner that makes every birthday a special one.*

### materials

Scraps of assorted red prints for block centers

¼ yard each of assorted yellow, purple, orange, green, pink, and blue prints for blocks

¼ yard of tan print for blocks

Scrap of candy cane stripe for blocks

½ yard of yellow polka dot for appliqués, inner border, and binding

⅝ yard of bright blue print for outer border

Yellow embroidery floss

Scraps of fusing-adhesive material

1⅛ yards of backing fabric

37×44" of quilt batting

**Finished quilt top: 38×31"**
**Finished blocks: 7" square**

### Select the Fabrics
While this is a scrappy quilt, it was pieced in a controlled manner. Before cutting, the assorted prints were sorted into color groups of purple, green, pink, blue, yellow, and orange.

Each of the four candle blocks utilized pieces from just one color group. For each Log Cabin block, the pieces in a color group were separated by light and dark.

### Cut the Fabrics
To make the best use of your fabrics, cut the pieces in the order that follows in each section.

### Cut and Assemble the Log Cabin Blocks
From assorted red prints, cut:
- 8—1½" A squares

From assorted yellow, purple, orange, green, pink, and blue prints, cut:
- 8—1½" A squares
- 16—1½×2½" B rectangles
- 16—1½×3½" C rectangles
- 16—1½×4½" D rectangles

- 16—1½×5½" E rectangles
- 16—1½×6½" F rectangles
- 8—1½×7½" G rectangles

1. For one Log Cabin block you'll need one red print A square, and from assorted prints one A square and two B, two C, two D, two E, two F, and one G rectangle.

2. Referring to the Assemble the Log Cabin Blocks instructions, steps 1 and 2, on *page 64,* make a Log Cabin block by sewing together pieces A through G. The finished block should measure 7½" square, including the seam allowances. Repeat to make a total of eight Log Cabin blocks.

## Cut and Assemble the Candle Blocks

This project uses "Christmas by Candlelight" Pattern X, which is on *Pattern Sheet 2.* To use fusing-adhesive material for appliquéing, as was done in this project, follow the Cut the Fabrics instructions, steps 1 and 2, on *page 64.*

From *each* of the assorted purple, green, blue, and pink prints, cut:
- 1—1½" A square
- 2—1½×5½" E rectangles
- 2—1½×7½" G rectangles
- 1—1⅞" square, cutting it in half diagonally to make a total of 2 M triangles

*continued*

From tan print, cut:
- 8—1½×2½" B rectangles
- 8—1½×5½" E rectangles
- 4—2½×3½" L rectangles
- 8—1⅞" squares, cutting each in half diagonally to make a total of 16 M triangles

From candy cane stripe, cut:
- 4—1½×2½" B rectangles

From yellow polka dot, cut:
- 4—Pattern X

1. For a purple candle block you will need one yellow polka dot X piece, two purple print M triangles, two tan print M triangles, one purple print A square, two tan print B rectangles, one candy stripe B rectangle, one tan print L rectangle, two tan print E rectangles, two purple print E rectangles, and two purple print G rectangles.

2. Referring to the Assemble the Candle Blocks instructions, steps 1 through 5, on *pages 64* and *65,* make a candle unit.

3. Sew a purple print E rectangle to the top and bottom edges of the candle unit. Join a purple G rectangle to each side edge of the candle unit. Fuse the yellow polka dot X piece in place. The finished purple candle block should measure 7½" square, including the seam allowances.

4. Repeat steps 1 through 3, substituting pink, green, or blue print pieces for the purple print pieces, to make a total of four candle blocks, one in each colorway.

## Assemble the Quilt Center

Referring to the photograph on *page 67* for placement, lay out the blocks in three rows. Sew together the blocks in each row. Press the seam allowances in each row in one direction, alternating the direction with each row. Then join the rows to complete the quilt center. The pieced quilt center should measure 28½×21½", including the seam allowances.

## Cut and Add the Borders

The measurements for the border strips are mathematically correct. Before cutting your strips. measure your pieced quilt center and adjust the lengths accordingly.

From yellow polka dot, cut:
- 4—2½×42" binding strips
- 2—1½×28½" inner border strips
- 2—1½×23½" inner border strips

From bright blue print, cut:
- 2—4½×31½" outer border strips
- 2—4½×30½" outer border strips

1. Sew a long inner border strip to the top and bottom edges of the pieced quilt center. Then join a short inner border strip to each side edge of the pieced quilt center. Press all seam allowances toward the yellow polka dot inner border.

2. Sew one short outer border strip to the top and bottom edges of the pieced quilt center. Then join a long outer border strip to each side edge of the pieced quilt center to complete the quilt top. Press all seam allowances toward the bright blue outer border.

## Complete the Quilt

Layer the quilt top, batting, and backing according to the instructions in Quilter's Schoolhouse, which begins on *page 146.* Quilt as desired. The Log Cabin blocks were machine-quilted with variegated thread in the Ribbon Quilting Design (see *Pattern Sheet 2*), the candle blocks were stitched in the ditch, and the border was quilted in a large loose stippling design. Use the yellow polka dot 2½×42" strips to bind the quilt according to the instructions in Quilter's Schoolhouse.

# *the* LOG CABIN THROW

*Scrap-bag strips sewn into Log Cabin blocks make a coverlet that looks like a find from Grandma's attic. We washed this quilt immediately after quilting and binding it to give it a crumpled, antique look.*

## materials

Scraps of assorted dark red prints for
   block centers

3 yards total of assorted light prints
   for blocks

3½ yards total of assorted dark prints
   for blocks

½ yard of dark red print for binding

3⅜ yards of backing fabric

61×83" of quilt batting

**Finished quilt top: 55×77"**

## Cut the Fabrics

To make the best use of your fabrics, cut the pieces in the order that follows.

From assorted dark red prints, cut:
- 35—1½" A squares

From assorted light prints, cut:
- 35—1½" A squares
- 35—1½×2½" B rectangles
- 35—1½×3½" C rectangles
- 35—1½×4½" D rectangles
- 35—1½×5½" E rectangles
- 35—1½×6½" F rectangles
- 35—1½×7½" G rectangles

- 35—1½×8½" H rectangles
- 35—1½×9½" I rectangles
- 35—1½×10½" J rectangles

From assorted dark prints, cut:
- 35—1½×2½" B rectangles
- 35—1½×3½" C rectangles
- 35—1½×4½" D rectangles
- 35—1½×5½" E rectangles
- 35—1½×6½" F rectangles
- 35—1½×7½" G rectangles
- 35—1½×8½" H rectangles
- 35—1½×9½" I rectangles
- 35—1½×10½" J rectangles
- 35—1½×11½" K rectangles

From dark red print, cut:
- 7—2½×42" binding strips

## Assemble the Log Cabin Blocks

Using one of each light and dark print A through K piece, make one Log Cabin block according to the Assemble the Log Cabin Blocks instructions, steps 1 and 2, on *page 64*. The finished block should measure

*continued*

*Small Log Cabin blocks turned on point mix with holly berry appliqués to make a merry mantel covering. Adjust the number of blocks to fit the width of your fireplace mantel.*

## materials

⅛ yard of solid dark red for block centers

¼ yard total of assorted light prints for blocks

⅛ yard total of assorted dark green prints for blocks and appliqués

⅛ yard total of assorted dark red prints for blocks and appliqués

½ yard of tan print for blocks

¾ yard of dark green stripe for binding

Scraps of fusing-adhesive material

1⅜ yards of backing fabric

21×49" of quilt batting

11½" square, including the seam allowances. Repeat to make a total of 35 Log Cabin blocks.

## Assemble the Quilt Top

Referring to the photograph *above* for placement, lay out the 35 Log Cabin blocks in seven rows. Position the blocks so they form diagonal bands of color as shown. Sew together the blocks in each row. Press the seam allowances in one direction, alternating the direction with each row. Join the rows to complete the quilt top. Press the seam allowances in one direction.

## Complete the Quilt

Layer the quilt top, batting, and backing according to the instructions in Quilter's Schoolhouse, which begins on *page 146.* Quilt as desired. Use the dark red print 2½×42" strips to bind the quilt according to the instructions in Quilter's Schoolhouse.

**Finished quilt top: 14⅝×42¾"**
**Finished block: 5" square**

## Cut the Fabrics

To make the best use of your fabrics, cut the pieces in the order that follows. This project uses "Christmas by Candlelight" patterns Y and Z, which are on *Pattern Sheet 2.* To use fusing-adhesive material for appliquéing, as was done in this project, follow the instructions under "Cut the Fabrics" on *pages 63 and 64.*

From solid dark red, cut:
• 5—1½" A squares
From assorted light prints, cut:
• 5—1½" A squares
• 5—1½×2½" B rectangles

The Log Cabin Collection

- 5—1½×3½" C rectangles
- 5—1½×4½" D rectangles

**From assorted dark green prints, cut:**
- 5—1½×2½" B rectangles
- 5—1½×3½" C rectangles
- 12 of Pattern Y

**From assorted dark red prints, cut:**
- 5—1½×4½" D rectangles
- 5—1½×5½" E rectangles
- 12 of Pattern Z

**From tan print, cut:**
- 1—8×43¼" rectangle
- 3—5⅞" squares, cutting each in half diagonally for a total of 6 triangles

**From dark green stripe, cut:**
- 1—25" square, cutting it into enough 2½"-wide strips to total 140" in length (see "Cut Bias Strips" in Quilter's Schoolhouse, which begins on *page 146*).

## Assemble the Log Cabin Blocks

Using two each of pieces A through E, make one Log Cabin block according to the Assemble the Log Cabin Blocks instructions, steps 1 and 2, on *page 64*. The pieced block should measure 5½" square, including the seam allowances. Repeat to make a total of five Log Cabin blocks.

## Assemble the Mantel Scarf

1. Referring to the photograph *above,* lay out the five Log Cabin blocks and five of the tan print triangles in diagonal rows.

2. Sew together the block and triangle in each row. Press the seam allowances in one direction, alternating the direction with each row. Then join the rows, adding the remaining tan print triangle last. Press seam allowances in one direction.

3. Fuse two dark red print berries and two dark green print leaves to each tan triangle. Using matching thread, machine-zigzag-stitch the appliqué pieces in place.

4. Sew the tan print 8×43¼" rectangle to the long straight edge of the appliquéd triangles to make the mantel scarf top.

## Complete the Mantel Scarf

Layer the pieced mantel scarf top, batting, and backing according to the instructions in Quilter's Schoolhouse, which begins on *page 146*. Quilt as desired. These mantel scarf blocks were machine-quilted in the ditch. Use the dark green stripe 2½×140" bias strip to bind the mantel scarf according to the instructions in Quilter's Schoolhouse.

# HOME & BEYOND

*Wanting to create a one-of-a-kind quilt, designer Mabeth*

*Oxenreider had two things in mind when she began this project—*

*a strong desire to work with plaids and the memory of some*

*antique quilts—and the result is wonderful. The blocks she used*

*inspired the trio of new projects that follow.*

## *the* QUILT

### materials

⅛ yard of red plaid for chimneys

⅛ yard of dark yellow plaid for windows and doors

8 yards total of assorted light and dark plaids
   and stripes for blocks

¼ yard of dark plaid No. 1 for border

½ yard of dark plaid No. 2 for border

⅝ yard of dark plaid No. 3 for binding

4 yards of backing fabric

70×81" piece of quilt batting

Freezer paper

**Finished quilt top: 64×75"**
**Finished blocks: House, 7½" square; bordered**
   **House, 10" square; large star, 7×10";**
   **small star, 5×7"; Log Cabin, 7½" square**

Quantities specified for 44/45"-wide, 100% cotton fabrics. All measurements include a ¼" seam allowance unless otherwise stated.

### Cut and Assemble the Units

For this project, the cutting and assembly instructions have been divided into units (designated by the heavy black lines in Diagram 1, *page 74*). To make the best use of your fabrics, cut the pieces in the order listed in each section.

The measurements for the border strips are mathematically correct. You may wish to cut your strips longer than specified to allow for possible sewing differences.

### Cut and Piece the House Blocks

The patterns are on *Pattern Sheet 1.* (The numbers used in the diagrams and cutting instructions are for position only.) To make templates of the patterns, follow the instructions in Quilter's Schoolhouse, which begins on *page 146*.

*continued*

**Diagram 1**

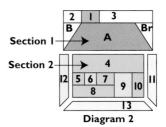

**Diagram 2**

From red plaid, cut:
- 10—1½×2" rectangles for position 1

From dark yellow plaid, cut:
- 10—1½" squares for position 6
- 10—2×2½" rectangles for position 9

From assorted light plaids and stripes, cut:
- 10 *each* of Pattern B and B reversed
- 10—1½×2" rectangles for position 2
- 10—1½×5" rectangles for position 3
- 10—1¼×4¾" rectangles for position 11
- 10—1¼×4¾" rectangles for position 12
- 10—1¼×8" rectangles for position 13

From assorted dark plaids and stripes, cut:
- 10 of Pattern A
- 10—2×6½" rectangles for position 4
- 10—1½" squares for position 5
- 10—1½×2" rectangles for position 7
- 10—1½×4" rectangles for position 8
- 10—1½×2½" rectangles for position 10

1. Referring to Diagram 2 for placement, lay out one each of pieces 1 through 13 and one each of patterns A, B, and B reversed in sections.

2. Sew together the pieces in each section. Add piece 13 to the bottom of Section 2, mitering the

corners according to the instructions in Quilter's Schoolhouse, which begins on *page 146*. Then join the sections to make a House block. The pieced House block should measure 8" square, including the seam allowances.

3. Repeat steps 1 and 2 to make a total of 10 House blocks. Set aside four house block units for the outer border.

## Assemble the Quilt Center

From assorted light plaids and stripes, cut:
- 36—2⅝" squares, cutting each in half diagonally for a total of 72 triangles

From assorted dark plaids and stripes, cut:
- 48—2⅝" squares, cutting each in half diagonally for a total of 96 triangles

1. Referring to Diagram 3, sew together three light plaid and stripe triangles and two dark plaid and stripe triangles, alternating dark and light, to make a border strip. Repeat to make a total of four border strips.

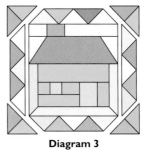

**Diagram 3**

2. Sew one pieced border strip to each edge of a House block. Press the seam allowances toward the border.

3. Sew together two dark plaid and stripe triangles in a pair. Repeat to make a total of four triangle pairs. Sew a triangle pair to each corner of a House block to make a bordered House block.

4. Repeat steps 1 through 3 to make a total of six bordered House blocks.

The Log Cabin Collection

**5.** Referring to Diagram 1 *opposite,* lay out the bordered House blocks in three horizontal rows. Sew together the blocks in pairs. Then join the pairs to make the quilt center. The pieced quilt center should measure 20½×30½", including the seam allowances.

## Cut and Add a Border

From dark plaid No. 1, cut:
- 2—1½×20½" strips
- 2—1½×32½" strips

Add one short border strip to the top and bottom edges of the pieced quilt center. Then sew a long border strip to each side edge of the quilt center. Press all seam allowances toward the border. The pieced quilt center should now measure 22½×32½", including seam allowances.

## Cut and Assemble the Flying Geese Border

From assorted light plaids and stripes, cut:
- 31—2½×4½" rectangles
- 62—2½" squares

From assorted dark plaids and stripes, cut:
- 31—2½×4½" rectangles
- 62—2½" squares

**1.** For accurate sewing lines, use a quilting pencil to mark the wrong side of each 2½" square with a diagonal line. (To prevent your fabric from stretching as you draw the lines, place 220-grit sandpaper under the squares.)

**2.** Referring to Diagram 4, with right sides together align one marked light square with one end of a dark 2½×4½" rectangle (note the placement of the marked line). Stitch on the marked line. Cut away the excess fabric, leaving a ¼" seam allowance. Press the attached triangle open. Repeat with a second marked light square, sewing it to the opposite end of the rectangle, to make a Flying Geese unit with dark center (see Diagram 5). Repeat to make a total of 31 Flying Geese units with dark centers.

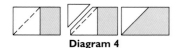

**Diagram 4**          **Diagram 5   Diagram 6**

**3.** Reversing the light and dark fabric positions, repeat Step 2 to make a total of 31 Flying Geese units with light centers (see Diagram 6).

**4.** For the left-hand border strip, sew together 16 Flying Geese units with dark centers in a vertical row (see Diagram 1 for placement). Join the strip to the left-hand edge of the pieced quilt center.

**5.** For the right-hand border strip, sew together 16 Flying Geese units with light centers in a vertical row. Join the strip to the right-hand edge of the pieced quilt center.

**6.** For the top border strip, sew together 13 Flying Geese units with dark centers in a horizontal row. Then sew together two units with dark centers. Join the pair, pointing up, to the left-hand end of the assembled strip. Join the strip to the top edge of the pieced quilt center.

**7.** For the bottom border strip, sew together 13 Flying Geese units with light centers in a horizontal row. Then sew together two units with light centers. Join the pair, pointing down, to the right-hand end of the assembled strip. Join the strip to the bottom edge of the pieced quilt center. The pieced quilt center should now measure 30½×40½", including the seam allowances.

## Cut and Add a Border

From dark plaid No. 2, cut:
- 2—3×30½" border strips
- 2—3×45½" border strips

Add a short border strip to the top and bottom edges of the pieced quilt center. Sew a long border strip to each side edge of the pieced quilt center. Press all seam allowances toward the border. The pieced quilt center should now measure 35½×45½", including the seam allowances.

## Cut and Assemble the Large Star Blocks

From assorted light plaids, cut:
- 15 *each* of patterns C, E, G, K, and M

From assorted dark plaids, cut:
- 15 *each* of patterns D, F, H, I, J, and L

**1.** Referring to Diagram 7, lay out one each of patterns C through M in three sections.

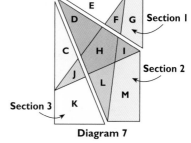

**Diagram 7**

*continued*

**2.** Sew together the pieces in each section. Then join the sections to make a large star block. The pieced large star block should measure 7½×10½", including the seam allowances.

**3.** Repeat steps 1 and 2 to make a total of 15 large star blocks.

## Cut and Assemble the Small Star Blocks

From assorted light plaids, cut:
- 9 *each* of patterns N, P, T, V, and X

From assorted dark plaids, cut:
- 9 *each* of patterns O, Q, R, S, U, and W

**1.** Referring to Diagram 8 lay out one each of patterns N through X in three sections.

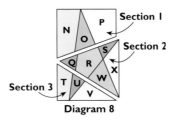

Diagram 8

**2.** Sew together the pieces in each section. Then join the sections to make a small star block. The pieced small star block should measure 5½×7½", including the seam allowances.

**3.** Repeat steps 1 and 2 to make a total of nine small star blocks.

## Assemble and Add the Star Border

**1.** Lay out one small star block and four large star blocks in a vertical row. Sew together the blocks to make a side border (see Diagram 1 on *page 74*). The pieced side border strip should measure 7½×45½", including the seam allowances. Repeat to make a second side border strip.

**2.** Sew the side border strips to the side edges of the pieced quilt center.

**3.** Lay out seven small star blocks in a horizontal row. Sew together the blocks to make the top border strip. The pieced top border strip should measure 5½×49½", including the seam allowances. Join the strip to the top edge of the pieced quilt center.

**4.** Lay out the remaining seven large star blocks in a horizontal row. Sew together the blocks to make the bottom border strip. The pieced bottom border strip should measure 10½×49½", including the seam allowances. Join to the bottom edge of the quilt center. The pieced quilt center should now measure 49½×60½", including the seam allowances.

## Cut and Assemble the Log Cabin Blocks

From red plaid, cut:
- 28—1¼" squares for position 1

From assorted light plaids and stripes, cut:
- 28—1¼" squares for position 2
- 28—1¼×2" rectangles for position 3
- 28—1¼×2¾" rectangles for position 6
- 28—1¼×3½" rectangles for position 7
- 28—1¼×4¼" rectangles for position 10
- 28—1¼×5" rectangles for position 11
- 28—1¼×5¾" rectangles for position 14
- 28—1¼×6½" rectangles for position 15

From assorted dark plaids and stripes, cut:
- 28—1¼×2" rectangles for position 4
- 28—1¼×2¾" rectangles for position 5
- 28—1¼×3½" rectangles for position 8
- 28—1¼×4¼" rectangles for position 9
- 28—1¼×5" rectangles for position 12
- 28—1¼×5¾" rectangles for position 13
- 28—1¼×6½" rectangles for position 16
- 28—1¼×7¼" rectangles for position 17
- 28—1¼×7¼" rectangles for position 18
- 28—1¼×8" rectangles for position 19
- 12—1¹⁄₁₆×8" rectangles for border

**1.** For one Log Cabin block you'll need one piece each for positions 1 through 19 (see Diagram 9).

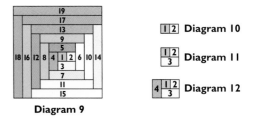

Diagram 9

**2.** For the block center, sew together the red plaid square 1 and the light square 2 (see Diagram 10). Press the seam allowance toward square 2.

**3.** Referring to Diagram 11, with right sides together align rectangle 3 with a long edge of the block center. Join the pieces. Press the seam allowance toward rectangle 3.

The Log Cabin Collection

**4.** Referring to Diagram 12 *opposite*, add rectangle 4 to the assembled pieces. Press the seam allowance toward the outside of the block.

**5.** Add rectangle 5 and press away from the center as before. Continue adding rectangles in numerical sequence, pressing toward the outside of the block, until the Log Cabin block is completed. The pieced Log Cabin block should measure 8" square, including seam allowances.

**6.** Repeat steps 1 through 5 to make a total of 28 Log Cabin blocks.

## Assemble and Add the Log Cabin Border

**1.** Referring to Diagram 13 pair two Log Cabin blocks along their dark edges; sew together. Repeat to make a total of eight Log Cabin pairs.

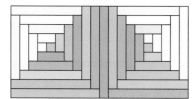

**Diagram 13**

**2.** Referring to Diagram 1 on *page 74*, join four Log Cabin pairs in a vertical row to make a side border strip. The pieced side border strip should measure 8×60½", including the seam allowances. Repeat to make a second side border strip.

**3.** Join the pieced side border strips to the side edges of the pieced quilt center.

**4.** Referring to Diagram 1, lay out six Log Cabin blocks, six dark 1¹⁄₁₆×8" border rectangles, and two pieced House blocks. Sew two border rectangles between paired Log Cabin blocks (see Diagram 14).

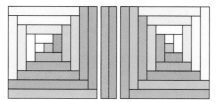

**Diagram 14**

**5.** Join the three pairs of Log Cabin blocks in a horizontal row. To each end of the horizontal row, sew a House block. The pieced top border strip should measure 8×64½", including the seam allowances. Join the strip to the top edge of the pieced quilt center.

**6.** Repeat steps 4 and 5 to make the bottom border strip. Sew the bottom border strip to the bottom edge of the pieced quilt center to complete the quilt top.

## Complete the Quilt

From dark plaid No. 3, cut:
- 7—2½×42" binding strips

Layer the quilt top, batting, and backing according to the instructions in Quilter's Schoolhouse, which begins on *page 146*. The back of this quilt was pieced with extra star blocks and a variety of compatible fabrics. Quilt as desired. This quilt was hand-quilted. Use the dark plaid 2½×42" strips to bind the quilt according to the instructions in Quilter's Schoolhouse.

## *the* WALL QUILT

*Log Cabin blocks are paired with House blocks in this warm-tone wall quilt inspired by "Home & Beyond." If you wish, change the colors to complement your decorating scheme.*

**Finished quilt top: 28×35½"**

### Cut the Fabrics

To make the best use of your fabrics, cut the pieces in the order that follows in each section.

This project uses "Home & Beyond" patterns, which are on *Pattern Sheet 1*. To make templates of the patterns, follow the instructions in Quilter's Schoolhouse, which begins on *page 146*.

## materials

2 yards total of assorted light and dark prints, plaids, and stripes for blocks, borders, and binding

⅛ yard of assorted dark yellow prints for blocks

1 yard of quilt backing

34×42" of quilt batting

### Cut and Assemble the House Blocks

From assorted dark prints, cut:
- 4—1½×2" rectangles for position 1
- 4 of Pattern A
- 4—2×6½" rectangles for position 4
- 4—1½" squares for position 5
- 4—1½×2" rectangles for position 7
- 4—1½×4" rectangles for position 8
- 4—1½×2½" rectangles for position 10

From assorted light plaids and stripes, cut:
- 4 *each* of patterns B and B reversed
- 4—1½×2" rectangles for position 2
- 4—1½×5" rectangles for position 3
- 4—1¼×4¾" rectangles for position 11
- 4—1¼×4¾" rectangles for position 12
- 4—1¼×8" rectangles for position 13

From assorted dark yellow prints, cut:
- 4—1½" squares for position 6
- 4—2×2½" rectangles for position 9

Referring to the Cut and Piece the House Blocks instructions on *page 74*, use one each of pieces 1 through 13 and one each of patterns A, B, and B reversed as shown in Diagram 2 to make a House block. Repeat to make a total of four House blocks.

### Cut and Assemble the Log Cabin Blocks

From assorted light plaids and stripes, cut:
- 8—1¼" squares for position 2
- 8—1¼×2" rectangles for position 3
- 8—1¼×2¾" rectangles for position 6
- 8—1¼×3½" rectangles for position 7
- 8—1¼×4¼" rectangles for position 10
- 8—1¼×5" rectangles for position 11
- 8—1¼×5¾" rectangles for position 14
- 8—1¼×6½" rectangles for position 15

From assorted dark plaids and stripes, cut:
- 8—1¼×2" rectangles for position 4
- 8—1¼×2¾" rectangles for position 5
- 8—1¼×3½" rectangles for position 8

- 8—1¼×4¼" rectangles for position 9
- 8—1¼×5" rectangles for position 12
- 8—1¼×5¾" rectangles for position 13
- 8—1¼×6½" rectangles for position 16
- 8—1¼×7¼" rectangles for position 17
- 8—1¼×7¼" rectangles for position 18
- 8—1¼×8" rectangles for position 19

**From dark yellow prints, cut:**
- 8—1¼" squares for position 1

Referring to the Cut and Assemble the Log Cabin Blocks instructions on *pages 76* and *77,* use one each of pieces for positions 1 through 19 to make a Log Cabin block. Repeat to make a total of eight Log Cabin blocks.

## Assemble the Quilt Center

Referring to the photograph *opposite* for placement, lay out the blocks in four horizontal rows.

Sew together the blocks in each row, pressing the seam allowances in one direction, alternating the direction with each row. Join the rows to make the quilt center. The pieced quilt center should measure 23×30½", including the seam allowances.

## Assemble and Add the Inner Border

1. Cut and piece assorted dark prints, plaids, and stripes to make the following:
   - 2—1¼×32" inner border strips
   - 2—1¼×23" inner border strips

2. Sew a short inner border strip to the top and bottom edges of the pieced quilt center. Then add a long inner border strip to each side edge of the quilt center. Press all seam allowances toward the inner border.

## Assemble and Add the Outer Border

From remaining assorted light and dark prints, plaids, and stripes, cut:
- 50—2½"-wide pieces varying in length from 2½" to 3½"

1. Randomly sew together enough assorted 2½"-wide pieces to make the following:
   - 2—2½×32" outer border strips
   - 2—2½×28½" outer border strips

2. Sew one long outer border strip to each side edge of the pieced quilt center. Then add a short outer border strip to the top and bottom edges of the pieced quilt center to complete the quilt top. Press all seam allowances toward the outer border.

## Complete the Quilt

From assorted dark prints, plaids, and stripes, cut and piece:
- Enough 2½"-wide strips to total 132" in length

Layer the quilt top, batting, and backing according to the instructions in Quilter's Schoolhouse, which begins on *page 146.* Quilt as desired. This quilt was machine-quilted with diagonal lines of wavy stitches.

Use the assorted dark print 2½"-wide pieced strip to bind the quilt according to the instructions in Quilter's Schoolhouse.

---

*the*
# FLOOR PILLOW

*Take a single House block from the "Home & Beyond" quilt and surround it with a border of Flying Geese for an inviting pillow that could be called Home Sweet Home.*

### materials

1½ yards total of assorted light and dark prints and plaids for blocks and borders

1½" square of dark gold print for block

⅛ yard of dark red plaid for inner border

1 yard of dark brown print for outer border and pillow backing

24" pillow form

**Finished pillow top: 24" square**

## Cut the Fabrics

To make the best use of your fabrics, cut the pieces in the order that follows.

This project uses "Home & Beyond" patterns, which are on *Pattern Sheet 1.* To make templates of the patterns, follow the instructions in Quilter's Schoolhouse, which begins on *page 146.*

*continued*

From light prints, cut
- 1—1½×2" rectangle for position 2
- 1—1½×5" rectangle for position 3
- 1—1¼×4¾" rectangle for position 11
- 1—1¼×4¾" rectangle for position 12
- 1—1¼×8" rectangle for position 13
- 6—2⅝" squares, cutting each in half diagonally for a total of 12 triangles
- 1 *each* of patterns B and B reversed
- 32—2½×4½" rectangles

From assorted dark prints, cut:
- 1—1½×2" rectangle for position 1
- 1 of Pattern A
- 1—2×6½" rectangle for position 4
- 1—1½" square for position 5
- 1—1½×2" rectangle for position 7
- 1—1½×4" rectangle for position 8
- 1—2×2½" rectangle for position 9
- 1—1½×2½" rectangle for position 10
- 8—2⅝" squares, cutting each in half diagonally for a total of 16 triangles
- 64—2½" squares

From dark gold print, cut:
- 1—1½" square for position 6

From dark red print, cut:
- 2—1½×10½" inner border strips
- 2—1½×12½" inner border strips

From dark brown print, cut:
- 2—2½×20½" outer border strips
- 2—2½×24½" outer border strips
- 1—24½" square for pillow back

## Assemble the Pillow Center

1. Referring to the Cut and Assemble the House Blocks instructions on *page 74,* use one each of pieces 1 through 13 and one each of patterns A, B, and B reversed to make a House block.

2. Referring to the Assemble the Quilt Center instructions, steps 1 through 3, on *page 74,* use 12 light print triangles and 16 dark print triangles to make a bordered House block.

## Assemble and Add the Borders

1. Sew one short inner border strip to each side edge of the bordered House block. Then add a long inner border strip to the top and bottom edges to make the pillow center. Press all seam allowances toward the dark red border.

2. Referring to the Cut and Assemble the Flying Geese Border instructions, steps 1 and 2, on *page 75,* use 32 assorted light print 2½×4½" rectangles and 64

assorted dark print 2½" squares to make 32 Flying Geese units.

3. Sew together six Flying Geese units in a horizontal row to make a pieced top border strip (see photograph *above*). The pieced top border strip should measure 4½×12½", including the seam allowances. Repeat to make the pieced bottom border strip. Join the pieced border strips to the top and bottom edges of the pieced pillow center.

4. Sew together eight Flying Geese units in a vertical row. Then sew together two additional units and join them, pointing left, to the bottom of the row to make a pieced side border strip (see the photograph *above*). The pieced side border strip should measure 4½×20½", including the seam allowances. Repeat to make a second pieced side border strip. Join the pieced side border strips to the side edges of the pieced pillow center.

5. Sew one short outer border strip to the top and bottom edges of the pieced pillow center. Then add a long outer border strip to each side edge of the pieced pillow center to complete the pillow front. Press all seam allowances toward the outer border.

## Assemble the Pillow

With right sides together, sew together the pieced pillow front and the dark brown print 24½" square pillow back, leaving an opening for the pillow form along a side edge. Turn the pillow cover right side out. Insert the pillow form through the opening. Whipstitch the opening closed.

# *the* FRAMED STARS

*Look no further than an old window sash for the perfect frame for "Home & Beyond" pieced stars. Adjust the block borders according to the size of the windowpane openings.*

**Finished block: 10×13"**

## Cut the Fabrics

To make the best use of your fabrics, cut the pieces in the order that follows. This project uses "Home & Beyond" pattern pieces, which are on *Pattern*

## materials

Scraps of assorted light and dark plaids and prints for blocks

¼ yard of black print for borders

Window sash with four panes (each of these openings measures 10×13")

Four 10×13" rectangles of self-sticking, acid-free, mounting board

*Sheet 1.* To make templates of the patterns, follow the instructions in Quilter's Schoolhouse, which begins on *page 146.*

## Cut and Assemble the Large Star Blocks

From assorted light plaids and prints, cut:
• *4 each* of patterns D, F, H, I, J, and L
From assorted dark plaids and prints, cut:
• *4 each* of patterns C, E, G, K, and M
From black print, cut:
• 16—2×10½" border strips

**1.** Referring to the Cut and Assemble the Large Star Blocks instructions on *pages 75* and *76,* use one each of patterns C through M to make a large star block.

**2.** Sew a black print border strip to each side edge of the star block. Then add one black print border strip to the top and bottom edges of the block. Press all seam allowances toward the black print border.

**3.** Repeat steps 1 and 2 to make a total of four large star blocks with borders.

## Frame the Star Blocks

Mount each star block to a 10×13", self-sticking, acid-free mounting board according to the manufacturer's directions. Insert in the openings of the window sash.

# AUTUMN SPLENDOR

*Bring to life the colors of fall in this patchwork project from quiltmaker Alice Berg. She gathered lots of fabrics in autumn hues, then assembled them into several traditional blocks to create this delightful sampler, which gave birth to the three new projects shown on the next few pages.*

## *the* QUILT

### materials

½ yard of solid tan for appliqué

¼ yard of solid sage green for appliqué

8" square of solid yellow for appliqué

¼ yard of solid rust for appliqué and border

½ yard of assorted gold prints for Flying Geese units

3 yards of solid black for Flying Geese units, borders, and binding

1¼ yards total of 20 assorted light prints for star blocks

1¼ yards total of 20 assorted dark prints for star blocks

1½ yards of brown-and-blue plaid for border

2½ yards of light brown print for borders

½ yard *each* of assorted scraps in green, blue, red, gold, bubble gum pink, purple, brown, and black for borders and Log Cabin blocks

¼ yard of red print for Log Cabin blocks

¼ yard of gold print for Log Cabin blocks

6 yards of backing fabric

86×102" of quilt batting

**Finished quilt top: 80×96"**
**Finished blocks: 8" square**

Quantities specified for 44/45"-wide, 100% cotton fabrics. All measurements include a ¼" seam allowance unless otherwise stated.

*continued*

## Cut the Fabrics

To make the best use of your fabrics, cut the pieces by sections as follows. The patterns are on *Pattern Sheet 1*. To make templates of the patterns, follow the instructions in Quilter's Schoolhouse, which begins on *page 146*.

## Appliqué the Center Block

Alice Berg was inspired to use this traditional appliqué block after seeing it in the book *Threads of Time* by Nancy J. Martin.

**From solid tan, cut:**
* 1—15½" square for center appliqué

**From solid sage green, cut:**
* 4 *each* of patterns D and E

**From solid yellow, cut:**
* 1 of Pattern A

**From solid rust, cut:**
* 2—1½×16½" border strips
* 2—1½×14½" border strips
* 4 of Pattern C
* 1 of Pattern B

1. To create positioning guides, fold the solid tan 15½" square in half diagonally twice and finger-press the folds. Referring to Diagram 1 for placement, baste the appliqué pieces onto the solid tan square.

**Diagram 1**

2. Using small slip stitches and threads that match the fabrics, appliqué the pieces in place. Trim the appliquéd square to 14½" square, which includes the seam allowances.

3. Sew a solid rust 1½×14½" border strip to the top and bottom edges of the appliquéd block. Then add a solid rust 1½×16½" strip to each side of the appliquéd block. Press all seam allowances toward the rust border.

## Cut and Assemble the Flying Geese Border

**From assorted gold prints, cut:**
* 32—2½×4½" rectangles for position F
* 4—4½" squares for position H

**From solid black, cut:**
* 80—2½" squares for position G

1. For accurate sewing lines, use a quilting pencil to mark each solid black square with a diagonal line on the wrong side of the fabric. (To prevent your fabric from stretching as you draw the lines, place 220-grit sandpaper under the squares.) Sixty-four of the black squares will be used for the Flying Geese units and 16 for the corner units.

2. With right sides together, align one marked solid black G square with one end of a gold print F rectangle (see Diagram 2; note the placement of the marked line). Stitch on the marked line. Trim the seam allowance to ¼". Press open the attached black triangle. In the same manner, sew a second solid black F square on the opposite end of the gold print G rectangle; trim and press open to make a Flying Geese unit (see Diagram 3). The Flying Geese unit should measure 2½×4½", including the seam allowances. Repeat to make a total of 32 Flying Geese units.

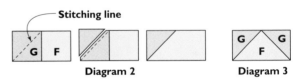

**Diagram 2**          **Diagram 3**

3. Referring to Diagram 4, align one marked solid black G square with one corner of a gold print H square (note the placement of the marked line). Stitch on the marked line. Trim the seam allowance to ¼". Press open the attached black triangle. Sew the remaining three marked solid black G squares to the remaining corners of the gold print H square in the same manner; trim and press to make a corner unit. The pieced corner unit should measure 4½" square, including the seam allowances. Repeat to make a total of four corner units.

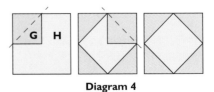

**Diagram 4**

**4.** To make one border strip, sew together eight Flying Geese units (see photograph on *page 82*). The pieced border strip should measure 4½×16½", including the seam allowances. Repeat to make a total of four border strips.

**5.** Sew a border strip to the top and bottom edges of the center block. Then add one corner unit to each end of the remaining two border strips. Sew a pieced border unit to each side edge of the center block. The center block should now measure 24½" square, including the seam allowances.

## Assemble and Add the Star Border

From *each* of 20 assorted light prints, cut:
- 4—2½×4½" rectangles
- 4—2½" squares

From *each* of 20 assorted dark prints, cut:
- 1—4½" square
- 8—2½" squares

**1.** For one star block you'll need one set of assorted light print pieces and one set of assorted dark print pieces.

**2.** Referring to the Cut and Assemble the Flying Geese Border instructions, steps 1 and 2, *opposite,* use a light print 2½×4½" rectangle and two dark print 2½" squares to make a Flying Geese unit. Repeat to make a total of four Flying Geese units.

**3.** Sew a Flying Geese unit to the top and bottom edges of the dark print 4½" square (see Diagram 5). Then add a light print 2½" square to each end of the remaining two Flying Geese units. Join one unit to each side edge of the dark print 4½" square to complete a star block. The pieced star block should measure 8½" square, including the seam allowances.

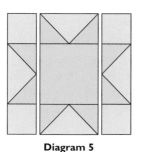

**Diagram 5**

**4.** Repeat steps 1 through 3 to make a total of 20 star blocks.

**5.** Set aside four star blocks for the outside border. Sew together the remaining star blocks in two rows of three blocks each and two rows of five blocks each.

**6.** Sew a short star block row to the top and bottom edges of the center block. Then add a long star block row to each side edge of the center block. The center block should now measure 40½" square, including the seam allowances.

## Assemble the Quilt Center

For this project the border strips are cut the length of the fabric (parallel to the selvage). The measurements for the border strips are mathematically correct. You may wish to cut your border strips longer than specified to allow for possible sewing differences.

From brown-and-blue plaid, cut:
- 2—3½×40½" border strips

From light brown print, cut:
- 2—2½×46½" border strips
- 2—2½×44½" border strips

From assorted print scraps, cut:
- 83—2½" squares
- 20—1½" squares

From solid black, cut:
- 2—2½×58½" border strips
- 2—3½×48½" border strips

**1.** Sew one brown-and-blue plaid 3½×40½" border strip to the top and bottom edges of the center block. Then add one light brown print 2½×46½" border strip to each side edge of the center block. Press all seam allowances toward the light brown and brown-and-blue plaid border.

**2.** Referring to Diagram 6, sew together four assorted print 1½" squares to make a Four-Patch unit. The pieced Four-Patch unit should measure 2½" square, including the seam allowances. Repeat to make a total of five Four-Patch units.

**Diagram 6**

**3.** Referring to the photograph on *page 82*, lay out the five Four-Patch units and the 83 assorted 2½" squares in four horizontal rows of 22 squares each. Join the squares in each row to make four pieced border strips.

*continued*

**4.** Sew two pieced border strips to the top and bottom edges of the center block.

**5.** Sew one light brown print 2½x44½" border strip to the top and bottom edges of the center block. Press the seam allowances toward the border.

**6.** Sew one solid black 2½x58½" border strip to each side edge of the center block. Then add one solid black 3½x48½" border strip to the top and bottom edges of the center block to complete the quilt center. Press all seam allowances toward the black border. The pieced quilt center should measure 48½x64½", including seam allowances.

## Assemble and Add the Log Cabin Block Border

From red print, cut:
- 16—2⅞" squares, cutting each in half diagonally for a total of 32 triangles

From gold print, cut:
- 16—2⅞" squares, cutting each in half diagonally for a total of 32 triangles

From assorted print scraps, cut:
- 384—1½"-wide strips of assorted lengths ranging from 3" to 8½"

**1.** Sew together one red print triangle and one gold print triangle to make a triangle-square (see Diagram 7). Press the seam allowance toward the red print triangle. The pieced triangle-square should measure 2½" square, including the seam allowances. Repeat to make a total of 32 triangle-squares.

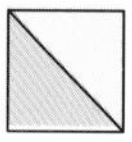

**Diagram 7**

**2.** With right sides together, align an assorted scrap 1½"-wide strip with one side edge of a triangle-square. (See Diagram 8, noting the position of the triangle-square.) Join the pieces. Trim the strip even with the triangle-square. Press the seam allowance toward the strip.

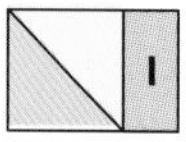

**Diagram 8**

**3.** Referring to Diagram 9, add an assorted scrap 1½"-wide strip to the top edge of the pieced block. Trim and press the strip as previously instructed.

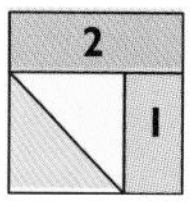

**Diagram 9**

**4.** Continue sewing strips to the center triangle-square in a counterclockwise direction, following the numerical sequence in Diagram 10, to complete a

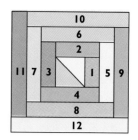

**Diagram 10**

Log Cabin block. Always press the seam allowance toward the outside of the block. The pieced Log Cabin block should measure 8½" square, including the seam allowances.

**5.** Repeat steps 2 through 4 to make a total of 32 Log Cabin blocks.

**6.** Sew together the Log Cabin blocks in four rows of eight blocks each.

**7.** Sew one Log Cabin row to each side edge of the quilt center. Then sew one Log Cabin row to the top and bottom edges of the quilt center. The pieced quilt center should now measure 64½x80½", including the seam allowances.

## Assemble and Add the Outer Border

From light brown print, cut:
- 2—2½x80½" strips
- 2—2½x64½" strips

From solid black, cut:
- 4—3½x80½" strips
- 4—3½x64½" strips

**1.** Join one solid black 3½x64½" strip to each long edge of a brown print 2½x64½" strip to make an outer border unit. Press the seam allowances toward the black strips. Repeat to make a second outer border unit. Sew the outer border units to the top and bottom edges of the pieced quilt center.

**2.** Join one solid black 3½x80½" strip to each long edge of a brown print 2½x80½" strip to make a side outer border unit. Press the seam allowances toward the black strips. Repeat to make a second side outer border unit. Sew a remaining star block to each end of the side outer border units. Press the seam allowances toward the border units. Sew one pieced side outer border unit to each side edge of the pieced quilt center to compete the quilt top. Press the seam allowances toward the border.

## Complete the Quilt

From solid black, cut:
- 9—2½×42" binding strips

Layer the quilt top, batting, and backing according to the instructions in Quilter's Schoolhouse, which begins on *page 146*. Quilt as desired. An Oak Leaf Quilting Design and a Maple Leaf Quilting Design (see *Pattern Sheet 1*) were hand-quilted on this quilt's black and brown outer border strips. The leaves were connected with swirling lines. Other blocks were quilted in the ditch or outlined. Use the solid black 2½×42" strips to bind the quilt according to the instructions in Quilter's Schoolhouse.

# *the* APPLIQUÉ PILLOW

*Bring the essence of fall into your living space with a simple appliqué pillow. The center block of "Autumn Splendor" delightfully showcases your appliqué and quilting skills.*

## materials

½ yard of tan print for appliqué foundation

⅓ yard of plum print for appliqué and border

Scraps of brown print for appliqués

½ yard of solid plum for appliqué and cording

Scraps of solid dark brown for appliqué

20" square of quilt batting

20" square of backing fabric

17½" square of fabric for pillow back

2 yards of ¼" cording

17" square pillow form

**Finished pillow top: 17" square**
**Finished appliqué block: 14" square**

## Cut the Fabrics

This project uses "Autumn Splendor" patterns, which are on *Pattern Sheet 1*. To make templates of the patterns, follow the instructions in Quilter's Schoolhouse, which begins on *page 146*. To make the best use of your fabrics, cut the pieces in the order that follows.

From tan print, cut:
- 1—15½" square for appliqué foundation

From plum print, cut:
- 4 of Pattern D
- 2—2×17½" border strips
- 2—2×14½" border strips

From brown print, cut:
- 4 of Pattern E
- 1 of Pattern B

From solid plum, cut:
- 1—18" square, cutting it into enough 1½"-wide bias strips to total 84" (See Cut Bias Strips in Quilter's Schoolhouse, which begins on *page 146*, for specific instructions.)
- 1 of Pattern A

From solid dark brown, cut:
- 4 of Pattern C

*continued*

### Appliqué the Block

1. Referring to the Appliqué the Center Block instructions, steps 1 and 2, on *page 84*, use the tan print 15½" square and appliqué pieces A through E to make an appliquéd block.

2. Sew a plum print 2×14½" border strip to the top and bottom edges of the appliquéd block. Then add a plum print 2×17½" border strip to each side edge of the appliquéd block to make the pillow top. Press all seam allowances toward the plum print border.

### Complete the Pillow Top

Layer the pillow top, batting, and backing according to the instructions in Quilter's Schoolhouse, which begins on *page 146*. Quilt as desired. This pillow top was echo-quilted by hand.

### Finish the Pillow

1. Sew the 1½"-wide bias strips together end to end to make one long strip. Trim one end perpendicular to the side and fold 1½" to the wrong side. With the right side out, fold the bias strip in half lengthwise to make a cover. Insert the cording next to the folded edge, placing a cording end 1" from the cover's folded end. Using a machine cording foot, sew through both fabric layers right next to the cording.

2. With the cording on the right side of the pillow top, align raw edges. Using the machine cording foot, and starting 1½" from the cover's folded end, stitch the covered cording to the pillow top. Round the corners, making sure the corner curves match. As you stitch each corner, gently push the covered cording into place.

3. Once the cording is stitched around the edge of the pillow top, cut the end of the cording so that it will fit snugly into the folded opening at the beginning. The ends of the cording should abut inside the cording cover. Stitch the ends down and trim raw edges as needed.

4. With right sides together, sew together the pillow top and the 17½" square pillow back, leaving an opening for the pillow form along one edge. Turn right side out and insert the pillow form through the opening. Whipstitch the opening closed.

# *the* NAUTICAL QUILT

*Two blocks from "Autumn Splendor" are redone here with seagoing flair. A lighthouse print at the center of each star sets the scene; a nautical motif in the borders carries out the theme.*

## materials

¼ yard of tan print for star blocks

¼ yard of blue lighthouse print for star blocks

1 yard total of four different red prints for star and Log Cabin blocks and border

½ yard of light blue print for quilt center

¼ yard of light gold print for Log Cabin blocks

⅝ yard of blue print for Log Cabin blocks and binding

¼ yard of gold print for border

1¼ yards of navy blue nautical print for border

1½ yards of backing fabric

52" square of quilt batting

**Finished quilt top: 45½" square**
**Finished blocks: 8" square**

## Cut the Fabrics

To make the best use of your fabrics, cut the pieces in the order that follows.

## Cut and Assemble the Quilt Center

From tan print, cut:
- 16—2½×4½" rectangles
- 16—2½" squares

From blue lighthouse print, cut:
- 4—4½" squares (refer to the photograph, *opposite,* to correctly position lighthouse motifs within square)

From assorted red prints, cut:
- 32—2½" squares (4 sets of 8 matching squares)

From light blue print, cut:
- 1—12⅝" square, cutting it diagonally twice in an X for a total of 4 side setting triangles

- 1—8½" setting square
- 2—6⅝" squares, cutting each in half diagonally for a total of 4 corner setting triangles

1. For one star block you will need one lighthouse print 4½" square, four tan print 2½×4½" rectangles, four tan print 2½" squares, and eight red print 2½" squares.

2. Referring to the Assemble and Add the Star Border instructions, steps 2 and 3, on *page 85,* make a total of four star blocks. Each finished block should measure 8½" square, including the seam allowances.

3. Referring to the photograph at *right,* lay out the four star blocks, the light blue print setting square, four light blue print side setting triangles, and four light blue print corner setting triangles in three diagonal rows.

4. Sew together the blocks and triangles in each row. Press the seam allowances in one direction, alternating the direction with each row. Then join the rows, adding two of the corner setting triangles last, to make the quilt center. Press the seam allowances to one side. The quilt center should measure 23¼" square, including the seam allowances.

## Cut and Assemble the Log Cabin Block Border

The following measurements for border strips are mathematically correct. You may wish to cut your border strips longer than specified to allow for possible sewing differences.

### From assorted red prints, cut:
- 4—2×23¼" border strips
- 2—2⅞" squares, cutting each in half diagonally for a total of 4 small triangles
- 8—6⅝" squares, cutting each in half diagonally for a total of 16 large triangles (4 sets of 4 triangles)

### From light gold print, cut:
- 2—2⅞" squares, cutting each in half diagonally for a total of 4 small triangles
- 4—1½×4½" rectangles for position 5
- 4—1½×5½" rectangles for position 6
- 4—1½×5½" rectangles for position 7
- 4—1½×6½" rectangles for position 8

### From blue print, cut:
- 4—1½×2½" rectangles for position 1
- 4—1½×3½" rectangles for position 2

- 4—1½×3½" rectangles for position 3
- 4—1½×4½" rectangles for position 4
- 4—1½×6½" rectangles for position 9
- 4—1½×7½" rectangles for position 10
- 4—1½×7½" rectangles for position 11
- 4—1½×8½" rectangles for position 12

### From gold print, cut:
- 4—1¼×23¼" border strips

### From navy blue nautical print, cut:
- 4—9⅝×23¼" border strips

1. Referring to the Assemble and Add the Log Cabin Block Border instructions, steps 1 through 4, on *page 86,* use one red print small triangle, one light gold print small triangle, one light gold print rectangle for positions 5 through 8, and one blue print rectangle for positions 1 through 4 and positions 9 through 12 to make a Log Cabin block. Repeat to make a total of four Log Cabin blocks.

2. Join a red print large triangle to opposite sides of a Log Cabin block. Press the seam allowances toward the triangles. Sew a red print large triangle to the

*continued*

remaining two sides of the Log Cabin block to make a corner block. The corner block should measure 11⅞" square, including the seam allowances. Repeat to make a total of four corner blocks.

3. For a border unit, join one red print 2×23¼" border strip to one gold print 1¼×23¼" border strip, and one navy blue nautical print 9⅝×23¼" border strip (see the photograph on *page 89* for placement). Press the seam allowances to one side. Repeat to make a total of four border units.

4. Sew one border unit to the top and bottom edges of the pieced quilt center. Press the seam allowances toward the border.

5. To each end of the two remaining border units sew a corner block. Press the seam allowances toward the border units. Sew one border unit to each side edge of the quilt center to complete the quilt top. Press the seam allowances toward the center of the quilt.

## Complete the Quilt
From blue print, cut:
• 5—2½×42" binding strips

Layer the quilt top, batting, and backing according to the instructions in Quilter's Schoolhouse, which begins on *page 146*. Quilt as desired. This quilt was machine-quilted; a wave pattern was quilted in the setting blocks and diagonal lines were quilted in the nautical print outer border strips. The pieced blocks were stitched in the ditch. Use the blue print 2½×42" strips to bind the quilt according to the instructions in Quilter's Schoolhouse.

# *the* WOODSY QUILT

*Take a close look at "Autumn Splendor" and you'll see the Flying Geese border that inspired the pattern in this North Woods-style throw. In this version, rows and rows of Flying Geese units border wide strips of a nature-inspired print.*

## materials
½ yard of red-and-tan plaid for blocks

1⅜ yards of red plaid for blocks

⅜ yard of tan print for blocks

1 yard of black print for blocks and binding

½ yard of tan-and-white print for blocks

¼ yard of red-and-black print for blocks

½ yard of black nature print

1½ yards of red-and-black plaid for borders

2¾ yards of backing fabric

50×58" of quilt batting

**Finished quilt top: 44×52"**

## Cut the Fabrics
To make the best use of your fabrics, cut the pieces in the order that follows. There are no patterns; the letter and number designations are for position only. Cut the border strips lengthwise (parallel to the selvage). The measurements for the border strips are mathematically correct. You may wish to cut your border strips longer than specified to allow for possible sewing differences.

From red-and-tan plaid, cut,
- 6—4½" squares for position H
- 24—2½x4½" rectangles for position F

From red plaid, cut:
- 36—2½x4½" rectangles for position F
- 180—2½" squares for position G

From tan print, cut:
- 18—2½x4½" rectangles for position F
- 36—2½" squares for position G

From black print, cut:
- 18—2½x4½" rectangles for position F
- 36—2½" squares for position G
- 5—2½x42" binding strips

From tan-and-white print, cut:
- 18—2½x4½" rectangles for position F
- 36—2½" squares for position G

From red-and-black print, cut:
- 9—4½" squares for position H

From black nature print, cut:
- 2—6½x36" strips for rows 5 and 11

From red-and-black plaid, cut:
- 2—4½x36½" border strips
- 2—4½x52½" border strips

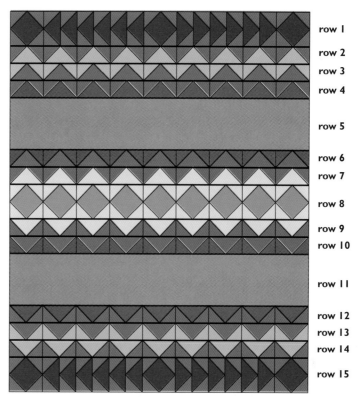

**Quilt Assembly Diagram**

row 1
row 2
row 3
row 4
row 5
row 6
row 7
row 8
row 9
row 10
row 11
row 12
row 13
row 14
row 15

## Assemble the Rows

Referring to the Cut and Assemble the Flying Geese Border instructions, steps 1 through 3, on *page 84*, assemble the following units.

**Row 1:** Make twelve Flying Geese units using 12 red-and-tan plaid F rectangles and 24 red plaid G squares. Make three corner units using three red-and-tan plaid H squares and 12 red plaid G squares. Lay out the units in a row as shown in the Quilt Assembly Diagram; sew together. Repeat to make Row 15.

**Row 2:** Make nine Flying Geese units using nine tan F rectangles and 18 red plaid G squares. Lay out in a row; sew together. Repeat to make Row 14.

**Row 3:** Make nine Flying Geese units using nine red plaid F rectangles and 18 tan G squares. Lay out in a row; sew together. Repeat to make Row 13.

**Row 4:** Make nine Flying Geese units using nine black F rectangles and 18 red plaid G squares. Lay out in a row; sew together. Repeat to make Row 12.

**Row 6:** Make nine Flying Geese units using nine red plaid F rectangles and 18 black G squares. Lay out in a row; sew together. Repeat to make Row 10.

**Row 7:** Make nine Flying Geese units using nine tan-and-white print F rectangles and 18 red plaid G squares. Lay out in a row; sew together. Repeat to make Row 9.

**Row 8:** Make nine corner units using nine red-and-black print H squares and 36 tan-and-white print G squares. Lay out in a row; sew together.

## Assemble the Quilt Center

Referring to the Quilt Assembly Diagram, lay out the 13 pieced rows plus the two black nature print 6½x36" strips. Sew together the rows to make the quilt center. Press the seam allowances in one direction. The pieced quilt center should measure 36½x44½", including the seam allowances.

## Add the Border

Sew one red-and-black plaid 4½x36½" border strip to the top and bottom edges of the pieced quilt center. Press the seam allowances toward the border. Join one red-and-black plaid 4½x52½" strip to each side edge of the pieced quilt center to complete the quilt top. Press the seam allowances toward the border.

## Complete the Quilt

Layer the quilt top, batting, and backing according to the instructions in Quilter's Schoolhouse, which begins on *page 146*. Quilt as desired. This quilt was machine-quilted with diagonal stripes in the center and with a pine motif in the borders. Use the black print 2½x42" strips to bind the quilt according to the instructions in Quilter's Schoolhouse.

# *the* INTERNATIONAL SPIRIT

*Foreign influences have been present in American quilting since the days when specialty fabrics were imported. As the 19th century began and America expanded its own textile industry, foreign goods became less prevalent. Now, quiltmakers in the United States are again inspired by international influences. Discover how fabrics and designs from faraway places are woven into 21st-century patchwork quilts.*

# ORIENT EXPRESS

*A graphic block arrangement and assorted large*

*Oriental prints add richness to this simple pattern. Project designer*

*Christine Brown collected her fabrics at quilt shops and*

*quilt shows across the country.*

## the QUILT

### materials

4¼ yards total of assorted light large-scale

    Oriental prints for blocks

2⅝ yards total of assorted dark large-scale

    Oriental prints for blocks

2⅔ yards of dark red print for border and binding

5⅔ yards for backing

79×95" of quilt batting

**Finished quilt top: 73×89"**
**Finished block: 8" square**

Quantities specified for 44/45"-wide, 100% cotton fabrics. All measurements include a ¼" seam allowance unless otherwise stated.

### Cut the Fabrics

To make the best use of your fabrics, cut the pieces in the order that follows. The pattern pieces are on *Pattern Sheet 2*. To make templates of the patterns, follow the instructions in Quilter's Schoolhouse, which begins on *page 146*.

Cut the binding and border strips lengthwise (parallel to the selvage). Extra length has been added to the border strips to allow for mitering the corners.

**From assorted light prints, cut:**
*   92 of Pattern A
*   48 *each* of patterns B and C
*   28 of Pattern E
*   16 of Pattern F

**From assorted dark prints, cut:**
*   112 of Pattern A
*   76 of Pattern B
*   48 of Pattern D
*   4 of Pattern F

**From dark red print, cut:**
*   4—2½×94" binding strips
*   2—5×94" border strips
*   2—5×78" border strips

*continued*

## Assemble the Blocks

*Block 1*

Referring to Diagram 1 for placement, lay out one light print A triangle, one dark print B piece, and one light print E piece; sew together to make a Block 1. Press the seam allowances toward the B piece. Pieced Block 1 should measure 8½" square, including the seam allowances. Repeat to make a total of 28 of Block 1.

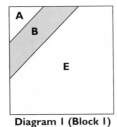

**Diagram 1 (Block 1)**

*Block 2*

Referring to Diagram 2 for placement, lay out one light print A triangle, two dark print A triangles, one light print B piece, one dark print B piece, one light print C piece, and one dark print D triangle in two sections.

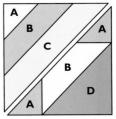

**Diagram 2 ( Block 2 )**

Sew together the pieces in each section. Then join the sections to make a Block 2. Pieced Block 2 should measure 8½" square, including the seam allowances. Repeat to make a total of 48 of Block 2.

*Block 3*

1. With right sides together and the long edges aligned, sew together a light print A triangle and a dark print A triangle to make a triangle-square. Press the seam allowances toward the dark print triangle. Repeat to make a total of four triangle-squares.

**2.** Referring to Diagram 3, lay out the four triangle-squares, one dark print F square, and four light print F squares in three horizontal rows. Sew together the pieces in each row. Press the seam allowances toward the light print squares. Then join the rows to make a Block 3. Press the seam allowances in one direction. Pieced Block 3 should measure 8½" square, including the seam allowances.

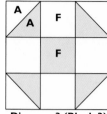

**Diagram 3 (Block 3)**

**3.** Repeat steps 1 and 2 to make a total of four of Block 3.

## Assemble the Quilt Top

**1.** Referring to the Quilt Assembly Diagram and the photograph on *page 96* for color placement ideas, lay out the blocks in 10 horizontal rows. Handle the blocks carefully to avoid stretching the bias edges. Rearrange the blocks until you're pleased with the color placement.

**2.** Sew together the blocks in each row. Press the seam allowances in one direction, alternating the direction with each row. Then join the rows to complete the quilt center. The pieced quilt center should measure 64½×80½", including the seam allowances.

| 3 | 1 | 1 | 1 | 1 | 1 | 1 | 3 |
|---|---|---|---|---|---|---|---|
| 1 | 2 | 2 | 2 | 2 | 2 | 2 | 1 |
| 1 | 2 | 2 | 2 | 2 | 2 | 2 | 1 |
| 1 | 2 | 2 | 2 | 2 | 2 | 2 | 1 |
| 1 | 2 | 2 | 2 | 2 | 2 | 2 | 1 |
| 1 | 2 | 2 | 2 | 2 | 2 | 2 | 1 |
| 1 | 2 | 2 | 2 | 2 | 2 | 2 | 1 |
| 1 | 2 | 2 | 2 | 2 | 2 | 2 | 1 |
| 1 | 2 | 2 | 2 | 2 | 2 | 2 | 1 |
| 3 | 1 | 1 | 1 | 1 | 1 | 1 | 3 |

**Quilt Assembly Diagram**

**3.** Add the long border strips to the side edges of the pieced quilt center and the short border strips to the top and bottom edges of the pieced quilt center, mitering the corners. For information on mitering, see the Mitered Border Corner instructions in Quilter's Schoolhouse, which begins on *page 146*.

## Complete the Quilt

Layer the quilt top, batting, and backing according to the directions in Quilter's Schoolhouse. This quilt was machine-quilted in the ditch along the block seams. Use the dark red print 2½×42" strips to bind the quilt according to the directions in Quilter's Schoolhouse.

## Orient Express Quilt
# *optional sizes*

If you'd like to make this quilt in a size other than for a twin bed, use the information *below*.

| Alternate Quilt Sizes | Wall | Full/Queen | King |
|---|---|---|---|
| **Number of blocks** | 36 | 99 | 169 |
| **Number of blocks wide by long** | 6×6 | 9×11 | 13×13 |
| **Number of No. 1 blocks** | 16 | 32 | 44 |
| **Number of No. 2 blocks** | 16 | 63 | 121 |
| **Number of No. 3 blocks** | 4 | 4 | 4 |
| **Finished size** | 57" square | 81×97" | 113" square |

### Yardage requirements

*Note: This quilt's borders and binding are cut from the same dark print and are cut lengthwise (parallel to the selvage). The border strips have extra length added to allow for mitering the corners.*

| | | | |
|---|---|---|---|
| Assorted light prints | 2 yards | 5¾ yards | 8½ yards |
| Assorted medium and dark prints | 1¼ yards | 4½ yards | 7¾ yards |
| Dark print | 1¾ yards | 3 yards | 3⅜ yards |
| Backing | 3¼ yards | 7¼ yards | 10 yards |
| Batting | 63" square | 87×103" | 119" square |

# *the* FALL-TONE QUILT

*This quilt illustrates the difference color placement makes. It utilizes just two "Orient Express" blocks, but one of those blocks is pieced in two slightly different color schemes. All three blocks fit together like a puzzle to form an eye-catching pattern.*

**Finished quilt top: 64" square**

## materials

1 5/8 yards of tan print for blocks

1 1/4 yards of green print for blocks

2 7/8 yards of brown print for blocks

5/8 yard of brown tone-on-tone print for blocks

5/8 yard of gold print for blocks and binding

1/2 yard of brown-and-tan print for blocks

3 7/8 yards of backing fabric

70" square of quilt batting

## Cut the Fabrics

To make the best use of your fabrics, cut the pieces in the order that follows. This project uses "Orient Express" pattern pieces, which are on *Pattern Sheet 2*.

To make templates of the patterns, follow the instructions in Quilter's Schoolhouse, which begins on *page 146*.

**From tan print, cut:**
- 24 of Pattern A
- 36 of Pattern B
- 20 of Pattern C

**From green print, cut:**
- 44 of Pattern B
- 16 of Pattern C

**From brown print, cut:**
- 20 of Pattern A
- 36 of Pattern D
- 24 of Pattern E
- 4—8½" squares

**From brown tone-on-tone print, cut:**
- 72 of Pattern A

**From gold print, cut:**
- 7—2½×42" binding strips
- 16 of Pattern A

**From brown-and-tan print, cut:**
- 16 of Pattern B

## Assemble the Blocks

**1.** Referring to the Assemble the Blocks, block 1, instructions on *page 96,* use one tan print A triangle, one green print B piece, and one brown print E piece to make a Block 1. Repeat to make a total of 24 of Block 1.

| Print | I | I | I | I | I | I | Print |
|-------|-----|-----|-----|-----|-----|-----|-------|
| I | 2A | 2A | 2A | 2A | 2A | 2A | I |
| I | 2A | 2B | 2B | 2B | 2B | 2A | I |
| I | 2A | 2B | 2B | 2B | 2B | 2A | I |
| I | 2A | 2B | 2B | 2B | 2B | 2A | I |
| I | 2A | 2B | 2B | 2B | 2B | 2A | I |
| I | 2A | 2A | 2A | 2A | 2A | 2A | I |
| Print | I | I | I | I | I | I | Print |

**Quilt Assembly Diagram**

**2.** Referring to the Assemble the Blocks, Block 2, instructions on *page 96,* use one brown print A triangle, one green print B piece, one tan print C piece, one tan print B piece, two brown tone-on-tone A triangles, and one brown print D triangle to make a Block 2A. Repeat to make a total of 20 of Block 2A.

**3.** Referring to the Assemble the Blocks, Block 2, instructions on *page 96,* use one gold print A triangle, one brown-and-tan print B piece, one green print C piece, one tan print B piece, two brown tone-on-tone A triangles, and one brown print D triangle to make a Block 2B. Repeat to make a total of 16 of Block 2B.

## Assemble the Quilt Top

Referring to the Quilt Assembly Diagram *left* and the photograph *above* for placement, lay out the blocks and four brown print 8½" squares in eight horizontal rows.

Sew together the blocks in each row. Press seam allowances in one direction, alternating the direction with each row. Then join the rows to complete the quilt top. Press the seam allowances in one direction.

## Complete the Quilt

Layer the quilt top, batting, and backing according to the instructions in Quilter's Schoolhouse, which begins on *page 146.* Quilt as desired. This quilt was machine-quilted with diagonal lines through the center of each block. Use the gold print 2½×42" strips to bind the quilt according to the instructions in Quilter's Schoolhouse.

# _the_ TABLETOP QUILT

_Who says scrappy quilts have to have a traditional look? This bright and lively tabletop-size quilt uses two "Orient Express" blocks in a medley of hot contemporary colors and patterns for sparkling results._

## materials

2¼ yards total of assorted dark blue and purple prints for blocks, border, and binding

⅔ yard total of assorted magenta prints for blocks and border

Scraps of assorted orange prints for blocks

⅛ yard total of assorted red prints for blocks

2⅔ yards of backing fabric

48" square of batting

**Finished quilt top: 42" square**

## Cut the Fabrics

To make the best use of your fabrics, cut the pieces in the order that follows. This project uses "Orient Express" pattern pieces, which are on _Pattern Sheet 2._ To make templates of the patterns, follow the instructions in Quilter's Schoolhouse, which begins on _page 146._

From assorted dark blue and purple prints, cut:
- 5—2½×42" binding strips
- 26—3½×6½" border rectangles
- 4—8½" squares
- 12 of Pattern A
- 4 _each_ of patterns B and C
- 8 of Pattern E

From assorted magenta prints, cut:
- 12 of Pattern B
- 30—2½-wide strips ranging in length from 4" to 8"

From assorted orange print scraps, cut:
- 8 of Pattern A

From assorted red prints, cut:
- 4 of Pattern D

## Assemble the Blocks

1. Referring to the Assemble the Blocks, Block 1, instructions on _page 96,_ use one dark blue or purple print A triangle, one magenta print B piece, and one dark blue or purple print E piece to make a Block 1. Repeat to make a total of eight of Block 1.

2. Referring to the Assemble the Blocks, Block 2, instructions on _page 96,_ use one dark blue or purple print A triangle, one magenta print B piece, one dark blue or purple print C piece, one dark blue or purple print B piece, two orange print A triangles, and one red print D triangle to make a Block 2. Repeat to make a total of four of Block 2.

## Assemble the Quilt Center

Referring to the Quilt Assembly Diagram _below_ for placement, lay out the blocks and the four dark blue or purple print 8½" squares in four horizontal rows.

Sew together the blocks in each row. Press the seam allowances in one direction, alternating the direction with each row. Then join the rows to complete the quilt center. Press the seam allowances in one direction. The pieced quilt center should now measure 32½" square, including seam allowances.

| Print | I | I | Print |
|-------|---|---|-------|
| I | 2 | 2 | I |
| I | 2 | 2 | I |
| Print | I | I | Print |

**Quilt Assembly Diagram**

## Add the Borders

1. Cut and piece the magenta print 2½"-wide strips to make the following:
   - 2—2½×36½" border strips
   - 2—2½×32½" border strips

2. Sew one short border strip to the top and bottom edges of the pieced quilt center. Then join one long border strip to each side edge of the pieced quilt center. Press all seam allowances toward the magenta border.

3. Sew together six dark blue or purple print 3½×6½" border rectangles in a vertical row to make a top border strip. The pieced top border strip should measure 3½×36½", including the seam allowances. Repeat to make the pieced bottom border strip. Sew the pieced top and bottom border strips to the top and bottom edges of the pieced quilt center.

4. Join seven dark blue or purple print 3½×6½" border rectangles in a vertical row to make a side border strip. The pieced side border strip should measure 3½×42½", including the seam allowances. Repeat to make a second side border strip. Sew the pieced side border strips to the side edges of the pieced quilt center to complete the quilt top. Press all seam allowances toward the outer border.

## Complete the Quilt

Layer the quilt top, batting, and backing according to the instructions in Quilter's Schoolhouse, which begins on *page 146*. Quilt as desired. This quilt's center and outer border were machine-quilted in an allover pattern; the magenta border was stitched in the ditch. Use the dark blue and purple print 2½×42" strips to bind the quilt according to the instructions in Quilter's Schoolhouse.

# WHEELS *of* WHIMSY

*Designers Wendy Hager and Shirlene Fennema combined*

*batik prints in circular pieced blocks to make this spirited quilt.*

*Their batik palette includes more than 100 different prints in colors*

*ranging from cool to warm, with a sprinkling of bright gold,*

*acid green, and hot pink fabrics for zest. Twelve complementary*

*batik prints compose the border and binding.*

## *the* QUILT

### materials

6 yards total of assorted batik prints for blocks

12—9×22" pieces (fat eighths) of assorted batik

    prints for border and binding *or* 1⅔ yards of

    a single batik print

3⅝ yards of backing fabric

64×76" of quilt batting

**Finished quilt top: 58×70"**
**Finished block: 6" square**

Quantities specified for 44/45"-wide, 100% cotton fabrics. All measurements include a ¼" seam allowance unless otherwise stated.

### Cut the Fabrics

To make the best use of your fabrics, cut the pieces in the order that follows. The patterns are on *page 109*. To make templates of the patterns, follow the instructions in Quilter's Schoolhouse, which begins on *page 146*.

From assorted batik prints, cut:
- 80 of Pattern A
- 33 of Pattern B
- 71 *each* of patterns C and C reversed
- 94 of Pattern D
- 9 of Pattern E

From *each* of the 12 assorted batik print fat eighths, cut:
- 1—5½×22" strip for border
- 1—2½×22" binding strip

*continued*

## Assemble the Blocks

*Block 1*

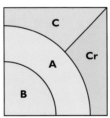

**Diagram 1**

1. Referring to Diagram 1 for placement, sew together one A piece and one B piece to make an A/B unit. Press the seam allowance toward the B piece.

2. Sew a C piece to a C reversed piece to make an C/C unit. Press the seam allowance open.

3. Join the A/B unit and the C/C unit to make a block 1. Press the seam allowance toward the C/C unit. Pieced block 1 should measure 6½" square, including the seam allowances.

4. Repeat steps 1 through 3 to make a total of 33 of block 1.

*Block 2*

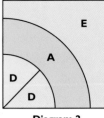

**Diagram 2**

1. Referring to Diagram 2, join two D pieces to make a D/D unit. Press the seam allowance open.

2. Sew together the D/D unit and an A piece to make an A/D/D unit. Press the seam allowance toward the D/D unit.

3. Join an E piece to the A/D/D unit to make a block 2. Press the seam allowance toward the E piece. Pieced block 2 should measure 6½" square, including the seam allowances.

4. Repeat steps 1 through 3 to make a total of nine of block 2.

*Block 3*

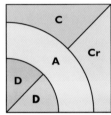

**Diagram 3**

1. Referring to Diagram 3, sew together two D pieces to make a D/D unit. Press the seam allowance open.

2. Sew together the D/D unit and the A piece to make an A/D/D unit. Press the seam allowance toward the D/D unit.

3. Sew together a C piece and a C reversed piece to make a C/C unit. Press the seam allowance open.

4. Sew together the A/D/D and C/C units to make a block 3. Press the seam allowance toward the C/C unit. Pieced block 3 should measure 6½" square, including the seam allowances.

5. Repeat steps 1 through 4 to make a total of 38 of block 3.

## Assemble the Quilt Center

1. Referring to the photograph *above left* for placement, lay out the blocks in 10 rows. Rearrange the blocks until you're pleased with the color placement.

2. Sew together the blocks in each row. Press the seam allowances in each row in one direction, alternating the direction with each row. Then join the rows to make the quilt center. Press the seam allowances in one direction. The pieced quilt center should measure 48½×60½", including the seam allowances.

## Add the Border

**1.** Cut and piece the 12 batik print 5½×22" strips to make the following:
- 2—5½×48½" border strips
- 2—5½×70½" border strips

**2.** Sew one short border strip to the top and bottom edges of the pieced quilt center. Press the seam allowances toward the border. Join one long border strip to each side edge of the pieced quilt center to complete the quilt top. Press all seam allowances toward the border.

## Complete the Quilt

Layer the quilt top, batting, and backing according to the instructions in Quilter's Schoolhouse, which begins on *page 146*. Quilt as desired. This quilt was machine-quilted with metallic variegated thread in a diagonal grid. Use the 12 batik print 2½×22" strips to bind the quilt according to the instructions in Quilter's Schoolhouse.

## the SMALL QUILT

*Just three colors—black, gray, and white—combine for this version of "Wheels of Whimsy." Any three shades of one color will work. Just piece 16 blocks and let the block arrangement work its magic.*

### materials

¾ yard of white print for blocks and border

⅝ yard of gray print for blocks and border

1 yard of black print for blocks and border

⅓ yard of solid black for binding

1⅛ yards of backing fabric

38" square of quilt batting

**Finished quilt top: 31½" square**

*continued*

## Wheels of Whimsy Quilt
# *optional sizes*

If you'd like to make this quilt in a size other than for a lap quilt, use the information *below*.

| Alternate Quilt Sizes | Wall | Twin | Full/Queen | King |
|---|---|---|---|---|
| **Number of blocks** | 30 | 117 | 168 | 289 |
| **Border width** | 2" | 5" | 5" | 5" |
| **Number of blocks wide by long** | 5×6 | 9×13 | 12×14 | 17×17 |
| **Finished size** | 34×40" | 64×88" | 82×94" | 112" square |
| | | | | |
| **Yardage requirements** | | | | |
| Assorted batiks for blocks | 2¼ yards | 6¾ yards | 9 yards | 15½ yards |
| Border—all one color | ⅓ yard cut crosswise | 2½ yards cut lengthwise | 2¾ yards cut lengthwise | 3¼ yards cut lengthwise |
| Binding | ⅓ yard | ⅝ yard | ⅔ yard | ⅞ yard |
| Backing | 1⅓ yards | 5¼ yards | 7⅓ yards | 9⅞ yards |
| Batting | 40×46" | 70×94" | 88×100" | 118" square |

## Cut the Fabrics

To make the best use of your fabrics, cut the pieces in the order that follows. This project uses the "Wheels of Whimsy" patterns, which are on *page 109*. To make templates of the patterns, follow the instructions in Quilter's Schoolhouse, which begins on *page 146*.

**From white print, cut:**
- 2—1×25½" inner border strips
- 2—1×24½" inner border strips
- 16 of Pattern A

**From gray print, cut:**
- 2—1¼×27" middle border strips
- 2—1¼×25½" middle border strips
- 4 *each* of patterns B, C, C reversed, and E
- 8 of Pattern D

**From black print, cut:**
- 2—3×32" outer border strips
- 2—3×27" outer border strips
- 4 *each* of patterns B, C, C reversed, and E
- 8 of Pattern D

**From solid black, cut:**
- 4—2½×42" binding strips

## Assemble the Blocks

*Block 3*

1. Referring to the Assemble the Blocks, Block 3, instructions on *page 104* and Diagram 4 *below,* use one white print A piece, one gray print C piece, one black print C reversed piece, one gray print D piece, and one black print D piece to make a block 3A. Repeat to make a total of four of block 3A. Pieced block 3A should measure 6½" square, including the seam allowances.

| Diagram 4 | Diagram 5 |
|-----------|-----------|

2. Referring to the Assemble the Blocks, Block 3, instructions on *page 104* and Diagram 5 *above,* use one white print A piece, one black print C piece, one gray print C reversed piece, one gray print D piece, and one black print D piece to make a block 3B. Repeat to make a total of four of block 3B. Pieced block 3B should measure 6½" square, including the seam allowances.

*Block 4*

1. Referring to Diagram 6, join a white print A piece and a black print B piece to make an A/B unit. Press the seam allowance toward the B piece.

2. Sew a black print E piece to the A/B unit to make a block 4A. Press the seam allowance toward the E piece. Pieced block 4A should measure 6½" square, including the seam allowances.

3. Repeat steps 1 and 2 to make a total of four of block 4A.

4. Referring to Diagram 7, join a white print A piece and a gray print B piece to make an A/B unit. Press the seam allowance toward the B piece.

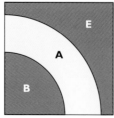
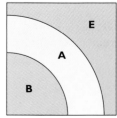

| Diagram 6 | Diagram 7 |
|-----------|-----------|

The International Spirit

**5.** Sew a gray print E piece to the A/B unit to make a block 4B. Press the seam allowance toward the E piece. Pieced block 4B should measure 6½" square, including the seam allowances.

**6.** Repeat steps 4 and 5 to make a total of four of block 4B.

## Assemble the Quilt Center

Referring to the photograph *opposite*, lay out the blocks in four rows. Rearrange the blocks until you're pleased with the color placement. Sew together the blocks in each row. Press the seam allowances in each row in one direction, alternating the direction with each row. Then join the rows to make the quilt center. Press the seam allowances in one direction. The pieced quilt center should measure 24½" square, including the seam allowances.

## Add the Borders

**1.** Sew one short inner border strip to the top and bottom edges of the pieced quilt center. Then add a long inner border strip to each side edge of the pieced quilt center. Press all seam allowances toward the white print border.

**2.** Sew a short middle border strip to the top and bottom edges of the pieced quilt center. Then add a long middle border strip to each side edge of the pieced quilt center. Press all seam allowances toward the gray print border.

**3.** Sew a short outer border strip to the top and bottom edges of the pieced quilt center. Then add a long outer border strip to each side edge of the pieced quilt center to complete the quilt top. Press all seams allowances toward the black print border.

## Complete the Quilt

Layer the quilt top, batting, and backing according to the instructions in Quilter's Schoolhouse, which begins on *page 146*. Quilt as desired. This wall hanging was machine-quilted. The circular pieces were quilted with circular scrolls; the leaf print at center and tree bark print in borders were quilted to replicate the shapes of the prints. Use the solid black 2½×42" strips to bind the quilt according to the instructions in Quilter's Schoolhouse.

# *the* AUTUMN THROW

*Mother Nature inspired the fabrics used in this fall-looking throw. To replicate this quilt, select fabrics from the dazzling array of natural-color botanical prints available, then sprinkle in a healthy dose of geometrics.*

## materials

4⅛ yards total of assorted light, medium, and dark autumn-color prints for blocks

1½ yards of dark red print for inner border and binding

1½ yards of dark green print for outer border

3 yards of backing fabric

52×64" of quilt batting

*continued*

**Finished quilt top: 46×58"**

## Cut the Fabrics

To make the best use of your fabrics, cut the pieces in the order that follows. This project uses the "Wheels of Whimsy" patterns, which are on *page 109*. To make templates of the patterns, follow the instructions in Quilter's Schoolhouse, which begins on *page 146*. The border strips are cut the length of the fabric (parallel to the selvage).

From assorted light, medium, and dark autumn-color prints, cut:
- 48 of Pattern A
- 21 of Pattern B
- 34 *each* of patterns C and C reversed
- 54 of Pattern D
- 14 of Pattern E

From dark red print, cut:
- 2—1½×48½" inner border strips
- 2—1½×38½" inner border strips
- 6—2½×42" binding strips

From dark green print, cut:
- 2—4½×50½" outer border strips
- 2—4½×46½" outer border strips

## Assemble the Blocks

Referring to the Assemble the Blocks instructions on *page 104*, use the light, medium, and dark autumn-color print A through E pieces to make 21 of block 1, 14 of block 2, and 13 of block 3.

## Assemble the Quilt Center

Referring to the photograph at *left*, lay out the 48 blocks in six horizontal rows. Rearrange the blocks until you're pleased with the color placement. Sew together the blocks in each row. Press the seam allowances in each row in one direction, alternating the direction with each row. Then join the rows to make the quilt center. Press the seam allowances in one direction. The pieced quilt center should measure 36½×48½", including the seam allowances.

## Add the Borders

1. Sew one long inner border strip to each side edge of the pieced quilt center. Then join one short inner border strip to the top and bottom edges of the pieced quilt center. Press all seam allowances toward the inner border.

2. Sew one long outer border strip to each side edge of the pieced quilt center. Then join one short outer border strip to the top and bottom edges of the pieced quilt center to complete the quilt top. Press the seam allowances toward the outer border.

## Complete the Quilt

Layer the quilt top, batting, and backing according to the instructions in Quilter's Schoolhouse, which begins on *page 146*. Quilt as desired. This quilt was machine-quilted with an allover curved leaf pattern. Use the dark red print 2½×42" strips to bind the quilt according to the directions in Quilter's Schoolhouse.

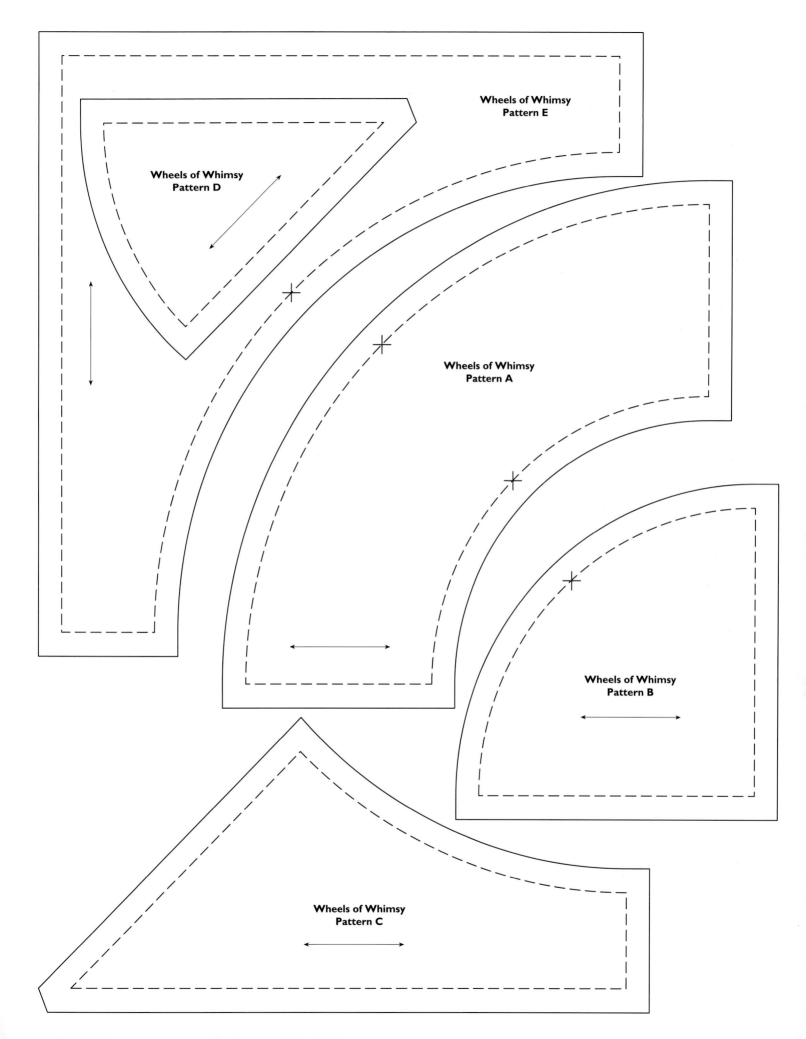

Wheels of Whimsy
Pattern E

Wheels of Whimsy
Pattern D

Wheels of Whimsy
Pattern A

Wheels of Whimsy
Pattern B

Wheels of Whimsy
Pattern C

# ENGLISH ELEGANCE

*A scrap bag filled with florals led designer Bettina Havig to create this charming quilt that elevates the humble Four-Patch to a new level when combined with a lovely chintz. A trio of offshoots—a throw, a table runner, and a wall quilt— grew from this bed-size quilt. See these projects on the pages that follow.*

## *the* QUILT

### materials

12—¼-yard pieces of assorted florals for blocks

5 yards of floral chintz for blocks, sashing, inner border, outer border, and binding

3 yards of light print for blocks

5½ yards of backing fabric

80×94" of quilt batting

**Finished quilt top: 74×88"**
**Finished block: 4×8"**

Quantities specified for 44/45"-wide, 100% cotton fabrics. All measurements include a ¼" seam allowance unless otherwise stated.

### Cut the Fabrics

To make the best use of your fabrics, cut the pieces in the order that follows. The patterns are on *Pattern Sheet 1.* To make templates of the patterns, follow the instructions in Quilter's Schoolhouse, which begins on *page 146.* The border and sashing strips are cut the length of the fabric (parallel to the selvage). These border strip measurements are mathematically correct. You may wish to cut your strips longer than specified to allow for possible sewing differences.

From assorted florals, cut:
- 256 of Pattern A
- 32—5¼" squares, cutting each diagonally twice in an X for a total of 128 triangles, *or* 128 of Pattern B

From floral chintz, cut:
- 2—6½×76½" outer border strips
- 2—6½×74½" outer border strips
- 3—6½×64½" sashing strips
- 2—2½×64½" inner border strips
- 2—2½×54½" inner border strips
- 8—2½×42" binding strips
- 130—2⅞" squares, cutting each in half diagonally for a total of 260 triangles, *or* 260 of Pattern D

From light print, cut:
- 64—4⅞" squares, cutting each in half diagonally for a total of 128 triangles, *or* 128 Pattern C
- 31—5¼" squares, cutting each diagonally twice in an X for a total of 124 triangles (you'll have two extra triangles), *or* 122 of Pattern B
- 4—3⅜" squares *or* 4 of Pattern E

### Assemble the Blocks

1. Referring to Diagram 1 for placement, sew together four floral A squares in two rows. Press the seam allowance in each row in one direction, alternating the direction with each row. Then join the rows to make a Four-Patch unit. Press the

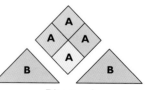

**Diagram 1**

*continued*

## Assemble the Block Rows

Referring to the photograph at *left* for placement, lay out the blocks in four vertical rows of 16 blocks each; sew together. Press the seam allowances in each row in one direction. Each pieced block row should measure 8½×64½", including the seam allowances.

## Assemble the Quilt Center

1. Mark 4" intervals on the wrong side of the three floral chintz 6½×64½" sashing strips.

2. Lay out the four block rows and three floral chintz sashing strips, alternating rows and strips. Sew together the rows, using the sashing strip marks as guides, to make the quilt center. Press the seam allowances toward the sashing strips. The pieced quilt center should measure 50½×64½", including the seam allowances.

## Add the Inner Border

Sew one long inner border strip to each side edge of the pieced quilt center. Then add a short inner border strip to the top and bottom edges of the pieced quilt center. Press all seam allowances toward the inner border. The pieced quilt center should now measure 54½×68½", including the seam allowances.

## Assemble and Add the Middle Border

1. Sew a floral chintz D triangle to one edge of a light print B triangle (see Diagram 3). Sew a second floral chintz triangle to the opposite edge of the light print B triangle to make a Flying Geese unit. Press the seam allowances toward the floral chintz triangles. The pieced Flying Geese unit should measure 4½×2½", including the seam allowances. Repeat to make a total of 122 Flying Geese units.

**Diagram 3**

2. Sew together 34 Flying Geese units in a vertical row to make a side middle border strip. Press the seam allowances in one direction. The pieced side middle border strip should measure 4½×68½", including the seam allowances. Repeat to make a second side middle border strip. Sew the side middle border strips to the side edges of the pieced quilt center.

3. Referring to Diagram 4, sew two floral chintz D triangles to opposite edges of a light print E square. Add two floral chintz D triangles to the remaining raw

**Diagram 4**

---

seam allowance in one direction. The pieced Four-Patch unit should measure 3½" square, including the seam allowances.

2. Sew a floral B triangle to the Four-Patch unit (see Diagram 1 on *page 111*). Then add a second floral B triangle to an adjacent edge. Press the seam allowances toward the floral B triangles.

3. Sew a light print C triangle to the pieced Four-Patch/B unit (see Diagram 2). Then add a second light print C triangle to the pieced Four-Patch/B unit to make a block. Press the seam allowances toward the light print C triangles. The pieced block should measure 8½×4½", including the seam allowances.

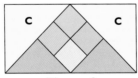

**Diagram 2**

4. Repeat steps 1 through 3 to make a total of 64 pieced blocks.

edges of the light print E square to make a corner block. Press the seam allowances toward the D triangles. The pieced corner block should measure 4½" square, including the seam allowances. Repeat to make a total of four corner blocks.

**4.** Sew together 27 Flying Geese units in a horizontal row. Add a corner block to each end of the row to make the top middle border strip. Press the seam allowances in one direction. The pieced top middle border strip should measure 4½×62½", including the seam allowances. Repeat to make the bottom middle border strip. Sew the top and bottom middle border strips to the top and bottom edges of the pieced quilt center. The pieced quilt center should now measure 62½×76½", including the seam allowances.

## Add the Outer Border
Sew one long outer border strip to each side edge of the pieced quilt center. Then add one short outer border strip to the top and bottom edges of the pieced quilt center to complete the quilt top. Press all seam allowances toward the outer border.

## Complete the Quilt Top
Layer the quilt top, batting, and backing according to the instructions in Quilter's Schoolhouse, which begins on *page 146.* Quilt as desired. Use the floral chintz 2½×42" strips to bind the quilt according to the instructions in Quilter's Schoolhouse.

# *the* TABLE RUNNER

*Traditional red, white, and blue prints give "English Elegance" a patriotic twist. It takes just eight blocks to make this table runner.*

## materials
¼ yard total of assorted Wedgwood blue prints

⅛ yard *each* of dark blue, gray, dark navy, and black prints

⅝ yard total of assorted white prints

½ yard of solid burgundy

⅜ yard of navy print

1½ yards of backing fabric

26×50" of quilt batting

**Finished table runner: 20×44"**

## Cut the Fabrics
To make the best use of your fabrics, cut the pieces in the order that follows. This project uses "English Elegance" patterns, which are on *Pattern Sheet 1.*

*continued*

113

## English Elegance Quilt
# *optional sizes*

If you'd like to make this quilt in a size other than for a double bed, use the information *below.*

| Alternate Quilt Sizes | Queen | King |
| --- | --- | --- |
| **Number of blocks** | 90 | 138 |
| **Number of Flying Geese** | 144 | 184 |
| **Number of pieced rows** | 5 | 6 |
| **Number of sashing rows** | 4 | 5 |
| **Finished size** | 88×96" | 102×116" |
| | | |
| **Yardage requirements** | | |
| Assorted florals | ¼ yard each of 12 | ¼ yard each of 16 |
| Floral chintz | 5¾ yards | 6¾ yards |
| Light print | 3 yards | 4 yards |
| Backing | 7⅞ yards | 9 yards |
| Batting | 94×102" | 108×122" |

To make templates of the patterns, follow the instructions in Quilter's Schoolhouse, which begins on *page 146*.

**From assorted Wedgwood blue prints, cut:**
- 4—5¼" squares, cutting each diagonally twice in an X for a total of 16 triangles, *or* 16 of Pattern B

**From *each* dark blue, gray, dark navy, and black print, cut:**
- 8 of Pattern A

**From white prints, cut:**
- 8—4⅞" squares, cutting each in half diagonally for a total of 16 triangles, *or* 16 of Pattern C
- 2—1½x10½" inner border strips
- 2—1½x32½" inner border strips
- 12—5¼" squares, cutting each diagonally twice in an X for a total of 48 triangles, *or* 48 of Pattern B

**From solid burgundy, cut:**
- 2—1½x12½" middle border strips
- 2—1½x34½" middle border strips
- 4—2½x42" binding strips

**From navy print, cut:**
- 48—2⅞" squares, cutting each in half diagonally for a total of 96 triangles, *or* 96 of Pattern D
- 4—4½" squares for outer border

## Assemble the Table Runner

1. Referring to the Assemble the Blocks instructions on *pages 111-112*, use four assorted dark blue, gray, dark navy, or black print A squares, two Wedgwood blue print B triangles, and two white print C triangles to make a block. Repeat to make a total of eight blocks.

2. Join the blocks in one vertical row.

3. Sew the long inner border strips to the long edges of the pieced block row. Then join the short inner border strips to the short edges of the pieced block row. Press all seam allowances toward the inner border.

4. Sew the long middle border strips to the long edges of the pieced block row. Then join the short middle border strips to the short edges of the pieced block row. Press all seam allowances toward the middle border.

5. Referring to the Assemble and Add the Middle Border instructions, Step 1, on *page 112*, use one white print B triangle and two navy print D triangles to make a Flying Geese unit. Repeat to make a total of 48 Flying Geese units.

6. Lay out two vertical rows of 18 Flying Geese units each. Sew together the units in each row to make two long pieced border strips. Press the seam allowances in one direction. Add the long pieced border strips to the long edges of the pieced block row.

7. Lay out two horizontal rows of six Flying Geese units each; sew together. Add a navy print 4½" square to each end to make two short pieced border strips. Press the seam allowances in one direction. Add the short pieced border strips to the short edges of the pieced block row to complete the table runner top.

## Complete the Table Runner

Layer the table runner top, batting, and backing according to the instructions in Quilter's Schoolhouse, which begins on *page 146*. Quilt as desired. This table runner was machine-quilted with a square grid. Use the solid burgundy 2½x42" strips to bind the table runner according to the instructions in Quilter's Schoolhouse.

# *the* FLYING GEESE THROW

*Combine the border from the "English Elegance" quilt with strips of plaid flannel to make this cozy throw. Use plaid flannel scraps to make the Flying Geese units in the outer border.*

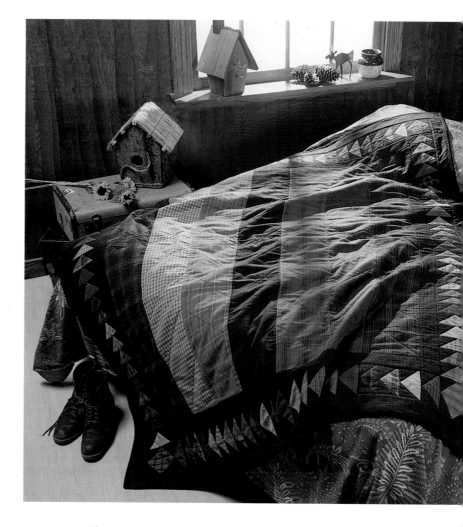

## materials

7—¼-yard pieces of assorted plaid flannels
    for quilt center

2 yards of dark blue plaid flannel for borders

⅝ yard total of assorted plaid flannel scraps
    for border

½ yard of solid black flannel for binding

3⅝ yards of 45"-wide quilt backing

64×76" of quilt batting

**Finished quilt top: 58×70"**

Quantities specified for 58/60"-wide, 100% cotton fabrics. All measurements include a ¼" seam allowance unless otherwise indicated.

## Cut the Fabrics

To make the best use of your fabrics, cut the pieces in the order that follows. This project uses "English Elegance" patterns, which are on *Pattern Sheet 1*. To make templates of the patterns, follow the instructions in Quilter's Schoolhouse, which begins on *page 146*. For this project, cut the border strips lengthwise (parallel to the selvage).

From *each* of seven assorted plaid flannels, cut:
- 1—6½×54½" strip

From dark blue plaid flannel, cut:
- 2—2½×66½" outer border strips
- 2—2½×58½" outer border strips
- 2—2½×54½" inner border strips

- 2—2½×46½" inner border strips
- 112—2⅞" squares, cutting each in half diagonally for a total of 224 triangles, *or* 224 of Pattern D

From assorted plaid flannels, cut:
- 26—5¼" squares, cutting each diagonally twice in an X for a total of 104 triangles, *or* 104 of Pattern B
- 4—3⅜" squares *or* 4 of Pattern E

From solid black flannel, cut:
- 5—2½×56" binding strips

## Assemble the Quilt Center

Sew together the seven plaid 6½×54½" strips as shown in the photograph *above* to make the quilt center. Press the seam allowances to one side. The quilt center should measure 42½×54½", including the seam allowances.

## Add the Inner Border

Sew one long inner border strip to each side edge of the pieced quilt center. Then join a short inner border strip to the top and bottom edges of the pieced quilt center. Press all seam allowances toward the inner border. The pieced quilt center should now measure 46½×58½", including the seam allowances.

*continued*

## Assemble and Add the Middle Border

1. Referring to the Assemble and Add the Middle Border instructions, Step 1, on *page 112*, use one plaid B triangle and two dark blue plaid D triangles to make a Flying Geese unit. The Flying Geese unit should measure 4½×2½", including the seam allowances. Repeat to make a total of 104 Flying Geese units.

2. Referring to the Assemble and Add the Middle Border instructions, Step 3, on *page 112*, use one plaid E square and four dark blue plaid D triangles to make a corner block. Repeat to make a total of four corner blocks.

3. Sew together 29 Flying Geese units in a vertical row to make a side middle border strip. Press the seam allowances in one direction. The pieced side middle border strip should measure 4½×58½", including the seam allowances. Repeat to make a second side middle border strip. Sew the side middle border strips to the side edges of the pieced quilt center.

4. Sew together 23 Flying Geese units in a horizontal row. Add a corner block to each end of the row to make the top middle border strip. Press the seam allowances in one direction. The pieced top middle border strip should measure 4½×54½", including the seam allowances. Repeat to make the bottom middle border strip. Sew the top and bottom middle border strips to the top and bottom edges of the pieced quilt center. The pieced quilt center should now measure 54½×66½" including the seam allowances.

## Add the Outer Border

Sew one long outer border strip to each side edge of the pieced quilt center. Then join one short outer border strip to the top and bottom edges of the pieced quilt center to complete the quilt top. Press all seam allowances toward the outer border.

## Complete the Quilt

Layer the quilt top, batting, and backing according to the instructions in Quilter's Schoolhouse, which begins on *page 146*. Quilt as desired. This quilt was machine-quilted through the center in a zigzag pattern; the Flying Geese units were outline-quilted. Use the solid black 2½×56" strips to bind the quilt according to the instructions in Quilter's Schoolhouse.

# *the* WALL QUILT

*Twenty "English Elegance" triangle units are the focal point of this wall quilt. Use a carefully orchestrated color scheme, as was done here, or a mix of scraps to make the Four-Patch block centers.*

## materials

⅜ yard of green print for blocks and inner border

¾ yard of red print for blocks and outer border

⅜ yard of tan print for blocks

1 yard of brown print for blocks, setting rectangles, and binding

1¼ yards of quilt backing

37×45" of quilt batting

**Finished quilt top: 31×39"**

## Cut the Fabrics

To make the best use of your fabrics, cut the pieces in the order that follows. This project uses "English Elegance" patterns, which are on *Pattern Sheet 1*. To make templates of the patterns, follow the instructions in Quilter's Schoolhouse, which begins on *page 146*.

From green print, cut:
- 40 of Pattern A
- 2—1½×34½" inner border strips
- 2—1½×24½" inner border strips

From red print, cut:
- 20 of Pattern A
- 5—5¼" squares, cutting each diagonally twice diagonally in an X for a total of 20 triangles, *or* 20 of Pattern B
- 2—3×39½" outer border strips
- 2—3×26½" outer border strips

From tan print, cut:
- 20 of Pattern A
- 5—5¼" squares, cutting each diagonally twice in an X for a total of 20 triangles, *or* 20 of Pattern B

From brown print, cut:
- 4—2½×42" binding strips
- 4—4½×8½" setting rectangles
- 20—4⅞" squares, cutting each in half diagonally for a total of 40 triangles, *or* 40 of Pattern C

## Assemble the Blocks

**1.** Referring to the Assemble the Blocks instructions on *pages 111-112*, use two green print A squares, one tan print A square, one red print A square, two tan print B triangles, and two brown print C triangles to make a block 1. Repeat to make a total of 10 of block 1.

**2.** Referring to the Assemble the Blocks instructions on *pages 111-112*, use two green print A squares, one tan print A square, one red print A square, two red print B triangles, and two brown print C triangles to make a block 2. Repeat to make a total of 10 of block 2.

## Assemble the Quilt Center

Referring to the Quilt Assembly Diagram *below* for placement, sew together the 20 blocks and the four brown print 4½×8½" setting rectangles in eight horizontal rows. Press the seam allowances in one direction, alternating the direction with each row. Then join the rows to make the quilt center. Press the seam allowances in one direction. The pieced quilt center should measure 24½×32½", including the seam allowances.

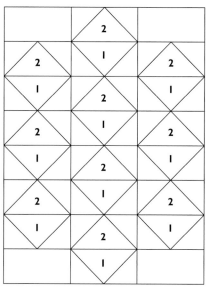

**Quilt Assembly Diagram**

## Add the Borders

**1.** Sew one short inner border strip to the top and bottom edges of the pieced quilt center. Then add one long inner border strip to each side edge of the pieced quilt center. Press all seam allowances toward the inner border.

**2.** Sew one short outer border strip to the top and bottom edges of the pieced quilt center. Then add one long outer border strip to each side edge of the pieced quilt center to complete the quilt top. Press all seam allowances toward the outer border.

## Complete the Quilt

Layer the quilt top, batting, and backing according to the instructions in Quilter's Schoolhouse, which begins on *page 146*. Quilt as desired. In this quilt, a square was machine-quilted in the center of each pieced block; the outer border was stitched in a large zigzag pattern. Use the brown print 2½×42" strips to bind the quilt according to the instructions in Quilter's Schoolhouse.

# the CHARM of APPLIQUÉ

Appliqué has its roots in the creative, elaborate

floral designs applied to cloth by stitchers in

colonial America. This decorative sewing technique

soon spread across the country, and reached its

pinnacle in the years preceding

the Civil War. The time-intensive

stitching method eventually gave

way in popularity to speedier

patchwork, but the allure

remained. The quilts and projects on the pages that

follow show contemporary adaptations of appliqué;

they can be stitched by hand or machine.

# HEAVEN & EARTH

*Quilt designer Marty Freed created this folk art wall hanging*

*of wool using simple appliqué shapes. Wool can be found today in nearly*

*every type of fabric store, including quilt shops. These appliqués are*

*so versatile they're used in later projects to embellish a vest,*

*a table runner, and another charming wall quilt.*

## *the* QUILT

**Finished quilt top: 51½×55½"**

Quantities specified for 44/45"-wide, 100% wool or cotton fabrics. All measurements include a ¼" seam allowance unless otherwise stated.

### Cut the Fabrics

Before cutting the wool for the appliqués, felt it so it won't run or ravel. To felt wool, machine-wash it in warm water with a small amount of detergent and machine-dry. If you choose to use wool from a piece of clothing, cut it apart and remove the seams before you felt it so it can shrink freely.

To make the best use of your fabrics, cut the pieces in the order that follows. The measurements for the border strips are mathematically correct. You may wish to cut your border strips longer than specified to allow for possible sewing differences. Cut the appliqué shapes to their finished sizes. No seam allowances are necessary because felted wool appliqués can be stitched in place without having to turn under the edges.

The patterns are on *Pattern Sheet 2*. To make templates of the patterns, follow the instructions in Quilter's Schoolhouse, which begins on *page 146*.

*continued*

## materials

1 yard of black-and-white print wool for appliqué

 foundation, border, and border corners

¾ yard of solid black wool for border

½ yard of solid turquoise felted wool for appliqués

 and border

⅞ yard of solid purple felted wool for appliqués

 and border

⅜ yard of solid green felted wool for appliqués

¼ yard of solid red felted wool for appliqués and border

⅛ yard of solid white felted wool for appliqués

 and border

¼ yard of solid burgundy felted wool for appliqués and

 border corners

¼ yard *each* of solid gold, solid bright blue, solid brown,

 and plaid felted wool for appliqués

3¼ yards of solid black flannel for backing and binding

58×62" of quilt batting

Perle cotton thread: gold, red, and black

From black-and-white print wool, cut:
- 1—22×26" rectangle for appliqué foundation
- 2—3×42" inner border strips
- 2—3×33" inner border strips
- 4—4⅜" squares

From solid black wool, cut:
- 2—6×33" strips for woven border
- 2—6×26" strips for woven border

From solid turquoise wool, cut:
- 2—2×45" middle border strips
- 2—2×38" middle border strips
- 1 of Pattern A
- 2 of Pattern F

From solid purple wool, cut:
- 2—6×45" outer border strips
- 2—6×41" outer border strips
- 1 of Pattern I

From solid green wool, cut:
- 1 *each* of patterns D, E, and E reversed
- 2 *each* of patterns H, M, CC, DD, and FF
- 12 of Pattern P

From solid red wool, cut:
- 4—1×27" strips for woven border
- 2 *each* of patterns G, N, and Q
- 1 *each* of patterns C, Z, and BB
- 3 of Pattern AA

From solid white wool, cut:
- 2—1×27" strips for woven border
- 3 of Pattern Q
- 2 of Pattern S
- 1 *each* of patterns V and V reversed

From solid burgundy wool, cut:
- 4—5⅛" squares, cutting each diagonally twice in an X for a total of 16 triangles
- 1 *each* of patterns J and J reversed

From solid gold wool, cut:
- 1 *each* of patterns B, K, Y, and AA
- 12 of Pattern O
- 5 of Pattern X
- 3 of Pattern Z

From solid bright blue wool, cut:
- 1 *each* of patterns L, L reversed, T, T reversed, U, and U reversed
- 3 of Pattern R

From solid brown wool, cut:
- 3 of Pattern S
- 2 of Pattern W
- 4 of Pattern EE

From plaid wool, cut:
- 4 of Pattern N
- 2 of Pattern R

From solid black flannel, cut:
- 6—2½×42" binding strips

## Appliqué the Center Section

1. Referring to the photograph on *page 120* for placement, arrange appliqué pieces A through L on the black-and-white print 22×26" appliqué foundation.

2. Using three strands of gold perle cotton thread, blanket-stitch around each piece to make the center section. (For specific instructions on blanket-stitching, see Quilter's Schoolhouse, which begins on *page 146*.)

   Using two strands of gold perle cotton thread, make three French knots in the center of each red G circle.

   To make a French knot (see diagram *below*), pull the thread through at the point where the knot is desired (A). Wrap the thread around the needle two or three times, unless otherwise stated, without twisting it. Insert the tip of the needle into the fabric at B, ¹⁄₁₆" away from A. Gently push the wraps down the needle to meet the fabric. Pull the needle and trailing thread through the fabric slowly and smoothly.

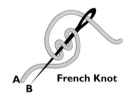

A  **French Knot**
B

The size of a French knot depends on the thickness of the thread and how many times you wrap it around the needle.

## Add the Woven Border

1. For the woven border you'll need two solid black 6×26" strips, two solid black 6×33" strips, four solid red 1×27" strips, two solid white 1×27" strips, and appliqué pieces M through P.

2. In each solid black 6×26" border strip, cut twelve 3"-wide slits approximately 2" apart, starting 2" from one end (see Diagram 1 *opposite*). Weave two solid red strips and one solid white strip through the slits in each black strip (see Diagram 2 *opposite*). Pin at each end. Make sure the ends are secure in the seam allowance.

3. Join a woven border strip to each side edge of the appliquéd center section. Press the seam allowances toward the woven border. Sew a solid black 6×33" border strip to the top and bottom edges of the appliquéd center section to complete

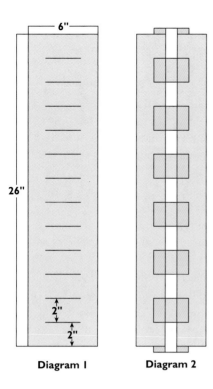

**Diagram 1**   **Diagram 2**

the quilt center. Press the seam allowances toward the black border.

4. Referring to the photograph on *page 120,* arrange appliqué pieces M through P on the top and bottom solid black border strips.

5. Using three strands of gold perle cotton thread, blanket-stitch around each piece. Using two strands of black perle cotton thread, satin-stitch the center of each gold O circle (see diagram *below*).

**Satin Stitch**

## Add the Borders

1. Sew a black-and-white print 3×33" inner border strip to the top and bottom edges of the quilt center. Then add one black-and-white print 3×42" inner border strip to each side edge of the quilt center. Press the seam allowances toward the black-and-white print border.

2. Sew a solid turquoise 2×38" middle border strip to the top and bottom edges of the quilt center. Then add a solid turquoise 2×45" middle border

strip to each side edge of the quilt center. Press the seam allowances toward the turquoise border.

3. Referring to Diagram 3, sew two solid burgundy triangles to opposite edges of a black-and-white print 4⅜" square. Press the seam allowances toward the triangles. Add a solid burgundy triangle to the square's remaining raw edges in the same manner to make a border block. The pieced border block should measure 6" square, including the seam allowances. Repeat to make a total of four border blocks.

**Diagram 3**

4. Sew a solid purple 6×41" outer border strip to the top and bottom edges of the quilt center. Press the seam allowances toward the purple border.

5. Sew a border block to each end of the solid purple 6×45" outer border strips. Press the seam allowances toward the solid purple strips. Sew a pieced border strip to each side edge of the quilt center to complete the quilt top. Press the seam allowances toward the solid purple border.

6. Referring to the photograph on *page 120* for placement, arrange the remaining appliqué pieces (Q through FF) on the solid purple borders.

7. Using three strands of gold or black perle cotton thread, blanket-stitch around each appliqué piece.

## Complete the Quilt

Layer the quilt top, batting, and backing according to the instructions in Quilter's Schoolhouse, which begins on *page 146.* Quilt as desired. The black-and-white print areas of this quilt were quilted in a meandering pattern. Use the solid black flannel 2½×42" strips to bind the quilt according to the instructions in Quilter's Schoolhouse.

## materials

Scraps of assorted prints in yellow, green,
    purple, pink, blue, and tan for appliqués

1½ yards of solid ivory for vest

1½ yards of light yellow print for lining

Tan perle cotton thread

Four assorted brown buttons

Two small purple buttons

Pattern for a lined vest without darts

½ yard of fusing-adhesive material

---

1. Lay fusing-adhesive material, paper side up, over the patterns. With a pencil, trace each pattern piece the number of times specified, leaving ½" between tracings. Cut out the pieces roughly ¼" outside of the traced lines.

2. Following the manufacturer's instructions, press the fusing-adhesive material shapes onto the backs of the designated fabrics; let cool. Cut out the shapes on the drawn lines. Peel off the paper backings.

**From assorted yellow prints, cut:**
- 1 *each* of patterns B, V, and X
- 2 of Pattern Z

**From assorted green prints, cut:**
- 1 *each* of patterns R and FF
- 2 of Pattern P

**From assorted purple prints, cut:**
- 1 *each* of patterns Q, T, U, and AA

**From assorted pink prints, cut:**
- 1 *each* of patterns N and AA

**From blue print, cut:**
- 1 of Pattern I

**From tan print, cut:**
- 1 of Pattern W

## Assemble the Vest

1. Trace the vest back pattern and one vest front pattern on the right side of the solid ivory. Turn the vest front pattern over and trace for the second front; do not cut out.

*the*
# VEST

*Sprinkle a few "Heaven & Earth" appliqué motifs on your favorite vest for a one-of-a-kind handmade garment.*

## Cut the Appliqués

To make the best use of your fabrics, cut the pieces in the order that follows. To use fusing-adhesive material for appliquéing, as was done on this project, complete the following steps. This project uses "Heaven & Earth" patterns, which are on *Pattern Sheet 2.*

**2.** Referring to the photographs *at left* for placement, arrange the appliqué pieces on the vest pieces.

**3.** Fuse the shapes in place with a hot, dry iron. Let the fabrics cool.

**4.** Using threads in colors that match the fabrics, machine-blanket-stitch or machine-zigzag-stitch around each appliqué shape.

## Complete the Vest

Pin the pattern pieces to the appliquéd vest tracings and cut out. Assemble the vest according to the pattern instructions.

Once assembled, use tan perle cotton thread and a large running stitch to hand-quilt ½" from the edges around the entire vest. Add the brown buttons to the center of the star appliqués and the purple buttons to the angel appliqué.

# the TABLE RUNNER

*For a twist on the "Heaven & Earth" quilt, make a table runner that uses just the borders and appliqués.*

## materials

½ yard of tan plaid for appliqué foundation

½ yard total of assorted gold prints for border and appliqués

¼ yard total of assorted red prints for border and appliqués

¾ yard total of assorted brown prints for border, appliqués, and binding

¾ yard total of assorted green prints for bias strips and appliqués

⅛ yard total of assorted blue prints for appliqués

⅛ yard of orange print for appliqués

1 yard of fusing-adhesive material

1¾ yards of backing fabric

31 x 54" of quilt batting

**Finished table runner: 25½×48"**

## Cut the Fabrics

To make the best use of your fabrics, cut the pieces in the order that follows. For this project, we used fusing-adhesive material for appliquéing. To use this same method, follow the Cut the Appliqués instructions, steps 1 and 2, *opposite*. This project uses "Heaven & Earth" patterns, which are on *Pattern Sheet 2.*

*continued*

**From tan plaid, cut:**
- 1—15×42½" rectangle for appliqué foundation

**From assorted gold prints, cut:**
- 2—6×42½" border strips
- 2 *each* of patterns B and C

**From assorted red prints, cut:**
- 2—1½×42" strips for border
- 2 of Pattern I
- 4 of Pattern N
- 24 of Pattern O

**From assorted brown prints, cut:**
- 4—2½×42" binding strips
- 2—1½×42" strips for border
- 2 of Pattern A
- 4 of Pattern G

**From assorted green prints, cut:**
- 1—18×42" rectangle, cutting and piecing it into two 1×50" bias strips (See Cut Bias Strips in Quilter's Schoolhouse, which begins on *page 146*.)
- 16 of Pattern P
- 2 *each* of patterns D, E, and E reversed
- 4 of Pattern H

**From assorted blue prints, cut:**
- 2 *each* of patterns C, L, J, and J reversed

**From orange print, cut:**
- 4 of Pattern F

## Piece and Appliqué the Center

1. Sew a gold print 6×42½" border strip to each side edge of the tan plaid 15×42½" rectangle to make the center section. Press the seam allowances toward the gold borders.

2. With wrong sides together, fold each green print 1×50" bias strip in half lengthwise; press. Machine-stitch ⅛" away from the raw edges along the entire length of the strips. Refold the strips, centering the stitched seams in the back, to make the vine appliqués; press.

3. Arrange the appliqué shapes on the center section. Pin the vine appliqués in place first, positioning pins away from the rest of the appliqué shapes.

4. Fuse all the appliqué shapes in place with a hot, dry iron. Let the fabrics cool.

5. Machine-blanket-stitch or machine-zigzag-stitch around the appliqué shapes with black thread.

## Add the Checkerboard Border

1. Aligning long edges, join one red print 1½×42" strip and one brown print 1½×42" strip to make a strip set. Press the seam allowance toward the brown print strip. Repeat to make a second strip set.

2. Cut the strip sets into a total of thirty-four 2"-wide segments.

3. Lay out 17 segments in a row; join the segments to make a checkerboard border strip. Press the seam allowances in one direction. Repeat to make a second checkerboard border strip.

4. Sew a checkerboard border strip to each short edge of the appliquéd center section to complete the table runner top. Press the seam allowances toward the table runner center.

## Complete the Table Runner

Layer the table runner top, batting, and backing according to the instructions in Quilter's Schoolhouse, which begins on *page 146*. Quilt as desired. This project was machine-quilted in the ditch. Use the brown print 2½×42" strips to bind the table runner according to the instructions in Quilter's Schoolhouse.

# *the* WALL QUILT

*Trees, birds, stars, and moon appliqué motifs from the "Heaven & Earth" quilt make a spirited wall hanging. Add the appliqués to the quilt by machine to complete the project quickly.*

**Finished quilt top: 30×36"**
**Finished block: 5" square**

## Cut the Fabrics

To make the best use of your fabrics, cut the pieces in the order that follows. For this project, we used fusing-adhesive material for appliquéing. To use this same method, follow the Cut the Appliqués

## materials

⅝ yard of gold print for blocks

⅝ yard of green plaid for blocks

¼ yard of black print for border

⅓ yard of dark green print for binding

Scraps of assorted green, gold, and brown prints
   for appliqués

I yard of fusing-adhesive material

I yard of backing fabric

36×41" of quilt batting

instructions, steps 1 and 2, on *page 124*. This project uses "Heaven & Earth" patterns, which are on *Pattern Sheet 2*.

From gold print, cut:
• 18—5½" squares
From green plaid, cut:
• 18—5½" squares
From black print, cut:
• 1—6½x30½" border rectangle
From dark green print, cut:
• 4—2½x42" binding strips
From assorted green prints, cut:
• 15 *each* of patterns CC and DD
From assorted gold prints, cut:
• 4 of Pattern B
• 5 of Pattern Z
• 1 *each* of patterns X, X reversed, and Y
From assorted brown prints, cut:
• 1 of Pattern L
• 2 of Pattern L reversed
• 30 of Pattern EE

## Assemble the Quilt

I. Referring to the photograph *above right* for placement, lay out the 18 gold print 5½" squares and the 18 green plaid 5½" squares in six horizontal rows, alternating colors. Sew together the blocks in each row. Press the seam allowances toward the green plaid squares. Then join the rows to make the quilt center. Press the seam allowances in one direction.

**2.** Sew the black print 6½x30½" border rectangle to the top edge of the pieced quilt center to complete the quilt top. Press the seam allowance toward the black rectangle.

**3.** Referring to the photograph, arrange the appliqué pieces on the pieced quilt top. Fuse the shapes in place with a hot, dry iron. Let the fabrics cool. Machine-blanket-stitch or machine-zigzag-stitch around the appliqué shapes with black thread.

## Complete the Quilt

Layer the quilt top, batting, and backing according to the instructions in Quilter's Schoolhouse, which begins on *page 146*. Quilt as desired. In this quilt, each green plaid square was machine-quilted with an X. The trees and birds were outline-quilted with gold thread and the black border rectangle was quilted in a meandering pattern that echoes the star and moon shapes. Use the dark green print 2½x42" strips to bind the quilt according to the instructions in Quilter's Schoolhouse.

# BEAUTY &VERLASTING

*Cindy Blackberg and Mary Sorensen work as a team*

*creating appliquéd quilts. Often their versions of the same project differ,*

*as illustrated by the first two renditions of this elegant wall quilt.*

*On the pages that follow you'll see other ways to use this pattern—*

*as a tabletop quilt and as a framed piece used in a serving tray.*

*Version 1 is Cindy's quilt.*

## the QUILT—VERSION 1

**Finished quilt top: 46" square**

Quantities specified for 44/45" wide, 100% cotton fabrics. All measurements include a ¼" seam allowance unless otherwise stated.

### Cut the Fabrics

To make the best use of your fabrics, cut the pieces in the order that follows. The patterns are on *pages 138 and 139*. To make templates of the patterns, follow the instructions in Quilter's Schoolhouse, which begins on *page 146*. Remember to add a ³⁄₁₆" seam allowance when cutting out each appliqué piece.

Cut the border strips the length of the fabric (parallel to the selvage). Extra length has been added to the border strips to allow for mitering the corners.

From cream print, cut:
- 1—18" square for appliqué foundation
- 2—18⅞" squares, cutting each in half diagonally for a total of 4 triangles for corner units
- 20 of Pattern V
- 4 of Pattern W
- 128 of Pattern X

*continued*

### Version I materials

1½ yards of cream print for appliqué foundation, sashing, corner units, and border

¼ yard of dark blue print No. I for appliqué and sunburst units

Scraps of assorted gold, tan, blue, dark green, and brown prints for appliqués, sashing, and border

Scraps of blue stripe for appliqués

¼ yard of black print for sunburst units

¼ yard of tan print for sunburst units

1¼ yards of dark blue tone-on-tone print for sashing and border

1⅜ yards of dark green print for sashing and border

⅜ yard of dark blue print No. 2 for binding

2½ yards of backing fabric

52" square of quilt batting

Gold embroidery floss

**From dark blue print No. 1, cut:**
- 1 of Pattern A
- 32 of Pattern R
- 8 *each* of patterns S and S reversed

**From assorted gold, tan, blue, dark green, and brown print scraps, cut:**
- 136 of Pattern X

**From assorted gold print scraps, cut:**
- 1 of Pattern B
- 4 of Pattern E
- 12 of Pattern H

**From assorted blue print scraps, cut:**
- 1 of Pattern C
- 4 *each* of patterns D and I

**From assorted dark green print scraps, cut:**
- 1—10" square, cutting it into enough ½"-wide bias strips to cut four 2¼"-long strips for position L and four 1¾"-long strips for position M (See Cut Bias Strips in Quilter's Schoolhouse, which begins on *page 146*, for specific instructions.)
- 4 *each* of patterns G, G reversed, J, and V
- 12 of Pattern K

**From blue stripe scraps, cut:**
- 4 of Pattern F

**From black print, cut:**
- 8 of Pattern Q

**From tan print, cut:**
- 40 of Pattern T

**From dark blue tone-on-tone print, cut:**
- 4—1½×41½" border strips
- 4—1½×22" sashing strips

**From dark green print, cut:**
- 4—3⅛×47½" border strips
- 4—3½×27½" sashing strips

**From dark blue print No. 2, cut:**
- 5—2½×42" binding strips

## Appliqué the Center

1. Fold the cream print 18" square appliqué foundation in half diagonally in both directions and lightly finger-crease to create position guidelines for appliqué.

2. Prepare all the appliqué pieces (patterns A–K) by basting under the 3⁄16" seam allowances; you don't need to turn under edges that will be overlapped by other pieces. For bias strips L and M, baste under a ⅛" seam allowance on the long edges.

3. Referring to the Center Appliqué Placement Guide on *page 139*, baste the prepared appliqué pieces to the foundation square. Begin with the pieces on the bottom and work up.

4. Using small slip stitches and threads that match the fabrics, appliqué the pieces to the foundation.

5. Using two strands of gold embroidery floss, backstitch details on the flowers (see Diagram 1).

**Diagram 1—Backstitch**

6. Trim the appliquéd square to 16½" square, which includes the seam allowances.

## Assemble the Sunburst Units

1. Sew together four dark blue print R pieces and five tan print T pieces, alternating colors and beginning and ending with a tan print piece to make a pieced arc (see Diagram 2). Join a dark blue print S triangle to one end of the pieced arc and a dark blue print S reversed triangle to the opposite end.

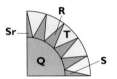

**Diagram 2**

2. With right sides together, pin the pieced arc to a black print Q piece. Place the first pin precisely at the center of the sewing line (see Diagram 3). Next place a pin at each end of the sewing line.

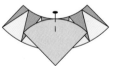

**Diagram 3**          **Diagram 4**

Then pin the remainder of the seam until all reference marks are matched and the pieces fit together smoothly (see Diagram 4). Sew together to make a sunburst unit. Press the seam allowance gently toward the black print piece.

3. Repeat steps 1 and 2 to make a total of eight pieced sunburst units.

## Assemble the Quilt Center

1. Place the template for cutting corners on the wrong side of the appliquéd 16½" square, ¼" from a corner (see Diagram 5 *opposite*). Trace around the template, transferring reference marks. Carefully cut ¼" inside the marked edge as shown in Diagram 6. Repeat in the remaining three corners of the appliquéd square.

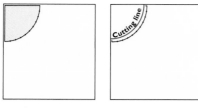

**Diagram 5**          **Diagram 6**

**2.** With right sides together, pin a sunburst unit to a cutout corner of the appliquéd square. Pin together as before; sew together. Join a sunburst unit to each remaining cutout corner of the appliquéd square in the same manner to make the quilt center. The pieced quilt center should still measure 16½" square, including the seam allowances.

## Assemble and Add the Sashing

**1.** Join one dark blue tone-on-tone print 1½×22" sashing strip and one dark green print 3½×27½" sashing strip, aligning long edges and the centers, to make a sashing strip set. Repeat to make a total of four sashing strip sets.

**2.** Add the sashing strip sets to the pieced quilt center with mitered corners. (For more information on mitering, see Quilter's Schoolhouse, which begins on *page 146*.) The pieced quilt center should now measure 24½" square, including the seam allowances.

## Assemble and Add the Pieced Triangle Sashing

**1.** Referring to Diagram 7, sew together 12 assorted print X triangles and 11 cream print X triangles in a row, alternating colors; sew a cream print V triangle to each end to make a triangle sashing strip. Repeat to make a total of four pieced triangle sashing strips.

**Diagram 7**

**2.** Join a pieced triangle sashing strip to the top and bottom edges of the pieced quilt center. Press the seam allowances toward the sashing.

**3.** Sew a cream print W square to each end of the remaining pieced triangle sashing strips (see Diagram 7). Sew a pieced triangle sashing strip to each side edge of the pieced quilt center. Press the seam allowances toward the sashing. The pieced quilt center should measure 26½" square, including the seam allowances.

## Assemble the Corner Units

**1.** Place the template for cutting corners on the wrong side of a large cream print triangle in the 90° corner. Mark and cut as before.

**2.** Sew a sunburst unit to the cutout edge of the triangle to make a pieced corner unit.

**3.** Repeat steps 1 and 2 to make a total of four pieced corner units.

**4.** Join a pieced corner unit to opposite edges of the pieced quilt center; add the remaining pieced corner units to the remaining edges of the quilt center to complete the pieced quilt top. The pieced quilt top should measure 37¼" square, including the seam allowances.

## Assemble and Add the Inner Border

**1.** Join one dark blue tone-on-tone print 1½×41½" border strip and one dark green print 3⅛×47½" border strip, aligning long edges and the centers, to make a border strip set. Repeat to make a total of four border strip sets.

**2.** Add the border strip sets to the pieced quilt top with mitered corners as before.

## Assemble and Add the Pieced Triangle Border

**1.** Referring to Diagram 8, sew together 22 assorted print X triangles and 21 cream print X triangles in a row, alternating colors; sew a cream print V triangle to each end to make a pieced triangle border strip. Repeat to make a total of four pieced triangle border strips.

**Diagram 8**

**2.** Join a pieced triangle border strip to the top and bottom edges of the pieced quilt top. Press the seam allowances toward the triangle border.

**3.** Join a cream print V triangle and a dark green print V triangle to make a triangle-square. The pieced triangle-square should measure 1½" square, including the seam allowances. Repeat to make a total of four triangle-squares.

*continued*

4. Sew a triangle-square to each end of the remaining pieced triangle border strips (see Diagram 8 on *page 131*).

5. Sew a pieced triangle border strip to each side edge of the pieced quilt top. Press the seam allowances toward the triangle border.

## Complete the Quilt

Layer the quilt top, batting, and backing according to the instructions in Quilter's Schoolhouse, which begins on *page 146*. Quilt as desired. This quilt was hand-quilted with a ½"-wide grid around the center appliqué, a cable design in the sashing, and a feather design surrounded by a ½" wide grid in the corner triangles. Use the dark blue print 2½×42" strips to bind the quilt according to the instructions in Quilter's Schoolhouse.

# *the* QUILT—VERSION 2

*Mary Sorensen's version of "Beauty Everlasting" differs from Cindy Blackberg's in color selection, the pieced triangle sashing, and the appliqué added to the corner units.*

**Finished quilt top: 46" square**

## Cut the Fabrics

To make the best use of your fabrics, cut the pieces in the order that follows. The patterns are on *pages 138 and 139*. To make templates of the patterns, follow the instructions in Quilter's Schoolhouse, which begins on *page 146*. Remember to add a ³⁄₁₆" seam allowance when cutting out each appliqué piece.

Cut the border strips the length of the fabric (parallel to the selvage). Extra length has been added to the border strips to allow for mitering the corners.

From tan print, cut:
- 1—18" square for appliqué foundation
- 2—18⅞" squares, cutting each in half diagonally for a total of 4 triangles for appliqué foundations

### Version 2 materials

1½ yards of tan print for appliqué foundations, sunburst units, sashing, and border

¼ yard of dark red print for appliqués and sunburst units

Scraps of assorted gold, olive green, red, orange, green, and dark green prints for appliqués, sashing, and border

½ yard of brown print for appliqués

½ yard of dark green print for sunburst units and binding

1¼ yards of black print for sashing and border

1⅜ yards of khaki print for sashing and border

2½ yards of backing fabric

52" square of quilt batting

Dark brown embroidery floss

- 32 of Pattern R
- 8 *each* of patterns S and S reversed
- 20 of Pattern V
- 128 of Pattern X

From dark red print, cut:
- 1 of Pattern A
- 8 *each* of patterns F and Q

From assorted gold print scraps, cut:
- 1 of Pattern B
- 12 of Pattern E
- 36 of Pattern H
- 4 of Pattern I
- 8 of Pattern J

From assorted olive green print scraps, cut:
- 12 *each* of patterns G and G reversed
- 64 of Pattern K
- 4 of Pattern W

From assorted red print scraps, cut:
- 1 of Pattern C
- 12 *each* of patterns D and I
- 4 *each* of patterns B and J

From assorted orange print scraps, cut:
- 4 of Pattern F

From assorted gold, green, and dark green print scraps, cut:
- 136 of Pattern X

**From brown print, cut:**

- 1—18" square, cutting it into enough ½"-wide bias strips to cut four 2¼"-long strips for position L, four 1¾"-long strips for position M, four 15"-long strips for position N, four 10½"-long strips for position O, and four 2½"-long strips for position P (See Cut Bias Strips in Quilter's Schoolhouse, which begins on *page 146* for specific instructions.)

**From dark green print, cut:**

- 5—2½×42" binding strips
- 40 of Pattern T

**From black print, cut:**

- 4—1½×41½" border strips
- 4—1½×22½" sashing strips

**From khaki print, cut:**

- 4—3⅛×47½" border strips
- 4—3½×27½" sashing strips

## Assemble the Quilt Center

1. To create the appliquéd center you need the tan print 18" appliqué foundation, one dark red print A piece, one gold print B piece, one red print C piece, four red print D pieces, four gold print E pieces, four orange print F pieces, four olive green print G pieces, four olive green print G reversed pieces, 12 gold print H pieces, four red print I pieces, four gold print J pieces, 12 olive green print K pieces, four brown print L strips, and four brown print M strips.

2. Referring to the Appliqué the Center instructions on *page 130*, steps 1 through 6, appliqué the tan print foundation square, except use dark brown embroidery floss for backstitching.

*continued*

3. Using pieces Q–T, the appliquéd 16½" square, and the sashing strips, assemble the sunburst units, quilt center, and sashing strip sets according to the instructions that begin on *page 130*. Add the sashing strip sets as directed to make the quilt center.

4. Using pieces V–X, follow the instructions under Assemble and Add the Pieced Triangle Sashing on *page 131*.

## Assemble and Appliqué the Corner Units

1. To appliqué one corner unit you need one pieced sunburst unit, one large tan print triangle, one red print B piece, one gold print C piece, two gold print E pieces, two dark red print F pieces, two olive green print G pieces, two olive green print G reversed pieces, six gold print H pieces, one gold print I piece, one red print I piece, one gold print J piece, one red print J piece, 13 olive green print K pieces, one brown print N strip, one brown print O strip, and one brown print P strip.

2. Follow the Assemble the Corner Units instructions on *page 131* to make a corner unit. Prepare the appliqué pieces as before; baste them to the pieced corner unit, referring to the Corner Appliqué Placement Guide on *page 138*. Using small slip stitches and dark brown embroidery thread, appliqué the pieces in place.

3. Repeat steps 1 and 2 to make a total of four pieced and appliquéd corner units.

## Add the Borders

Using the border strips and the remaining assorted print X triangles, complete the quilt top by assembling and adding the inner border and pieced triangle border according to the instructions on *pages 131 and 132*.

## Complete the Quilt

Layer the quilt top, batting, and backing according to the instructions in Quilter's Schoolhouse, which begins on *page 146*. Quilt as desired. This quilt was hand-quilted in a ½"-wide grid around the center appliqué and the corner unit appliqués. Use the dark green print 2½×42" strips to bind the quilt according to the instructions in Quilter's Schoolhouse.

# *the* TABLETOP QUILT

*This tabletop quilt is a simplified, pieced-only version of the "Beauty Everlasting" quilts. You'll recognize their corner units; they're used here as the centerpiece. The borders feature two rows of triangles.*

## materials

¼ yard of green print for block centers

1 yard of pink print for blocks and binding

1⅛ yards of light pink print for blocks, sashing, and border

⅝ yard of green floral for quilt center

1⅛ yards of backing fabric

38" square of flannel for quilt batting

**Finished quilt top: 32" square**

## Cut the Fabrics

To make the best use of your fabrics, cut the pieces in the order that follows. This project uses the "Beauty Everlasting" patterns on *pages 138 and 139*. To make templates of the patterns, follow the instructions in Quilter's Schoolhouse, which begins on *page 146*.

From green print, cut:
• 4 of Pattern Q
From pink print, cut:
• 4—2½×42" binding strips
• 16 of Pattern R
• 4 *each* of patterns S and S reversed
• 108 of Pattern X
• 8 of Pattern W
From light pink print, cut:
• 2—2½×30½" inner border strips
• 2—2½×26½" inner border strips
• 100 of Pattern X
• 20 of Pattern T
• 16 of Pattern V

From green floral, cut:

- 2—1⅞ squares, cutting each in half diagonally for a total of 4 triangles

## Assemble the Units

1. Referring to the Assemble the Sunburst Units instructions on *page 130,* use one green print Q piece, four pink print R pieces, one pink print S piece, one pink print S reversed piece, and five light pink print T pieces to make a sunburst unit. Repeat to make a total of four sunburst units.

2. Referring to the Assemble the Corner Units instructions, steps 1 and 2, on *page 131,* use a green floral triangle and one sunburst unit to make a corner unit. Repeat to make a total of four corner units.

## Assemble the Quilt Center

Lay out the four corner units in pairs with the sunburst units at the center. Sew together the pairs. Then, join the pairs to make the quilt center. Press seam allowances to one side. Trim the quilt center to 24½" square, including the seam allowances.

## Assemble and Add the Pieced Triangle Sashing

Follow the Assemble and Add the Pieced Triangle Sashing instructions on *page 131,* using pink print and light pink print pieces.

## Add the Inner Border

Sew one light pink print 2½×26½" inner border strip to the top and bottom edges of the pieced quilt

*continued*

center. Press the seam allowances toward the border. Join one light pink print 2½×30½" inner border strip to each side edge of the pieced quilt center. Press the seam allowances toward the inner border.

## Assemble and Add the Pieced Triangle Border

Follow the Assemble and Add the Pieced Triangle Border instructions on *page 131,* using pink print and light pink print pieces to complete the quilt top.

## Complete the Quilt

Layer the quilt top, flannel, and backing according to the instructions in Quilter's Schoolhouse, which begins on *page 146.* Quilt as desired. These borders were machine-quilted in the ditch. Use the pink print 2½×42" strips to bind the quilt according to the instructions in Quilter's Schoolhouse.

---

# *the* SERVING TRAY

*A serving tray lets you put a finished piece to work. Here the tray holds an appliquéd block surrounded by a pieced border.*

## materials

½ yard of tan print for appliqué background and border

Scraps of assorted red prints for appliqués

Scrap of gold print for appliqués

Scrap of black print for appliqués

Scrap of green print for appliqués

⅛ yard of dark green print for appliqués

⅓ yard of red-and-black print for border

Metallic gold machine embroidery thread

15×24" cherry wood frame

Two brass drawer pulls

Scraps of fusing-adhesive material

**Finished quilt top: 15×23"**

## Cut the Fabrics

To make the best use of your fabrics, cut the pieces in the order that follows. To use fusing-adhesive material for appliquéing, as was done in this project, complete the following steps. This project uses "Beauty Everlasting" patterns, which are on *pages 138 and 139.*

1. Lay fusing-adhesive material, paper side up, over the patterns. With a pencil, trace each pattern piece the number of times specified, leaving ½" between tracings. Cut out the pieces roughly ¼" outside of the traced lines.

2. Following the manufacturer's instructions, press the fusing-adhesive material shapes onto the backs of the designated fabrics; let cool. Cut out the shapes on the drawn lines. Peel off the paper backings.

From tan print, cut:
• 1—12×20½" rectangle
• 24 of Pattern X
• 8 of Pattern V

From assorted red print scraps, cut:
• 1 of Pattern B
• 1 of Pattern C
• 2 of Pattern D
• 2 of Pattern F
• 2 of Pattern I
• 2 of Pattern J

From gold print, cut:
• 2 of Pattern E

From black print, cut:
• 2 *each* of patterns G and G reversed
• 6 of Pattern H

From green print, cut:
• 12 of Pattern K

**From dark green print, cut:**
- ¼×15" bias strip for position N
- 2—¼×6" bias strips for positions O and P

**From red-and-black print, cut:**
- 2—2×23½" outer border strips
- 2—2×12½" outer border strips
- 28 of Pattern X
- 4 of Pattern W

## Appliqué the Center

**1.** Arrange the appliqué pieces on the tan print 12×20½" rectangle, referring to the Corner Appliqué Placement Guide on *page 138*. Fuse the shapes in place with a hot dry iron. Let the fabrics cool.

**2.** Machine-satin-stitch the appliqué pieces in place. Topstitch with metallic gold thread.

**3.** Trim the appliquéd rectangle to 10½×18½", which includes the seam allowances.

## Assemble and Add the Border

**1.** Referring to Assemble and Add the Pieced Triangle Border instructions, Step 1, on *page 131*, use four tan print X triangles, five red-and-black print X triangles, and two tan print V triangles to make a short border strip. Repeat to make a second short border strip.

**2.** Join a short border strip to each short edge of the appliquéd rectangle. Press the seam allowances toward the appliquéd rectangle.

**3.** In the same manner, join eight tan X triangles, nine red-and-black print X triangles, and two tan print V triangles into a triangle strip. Sew a red-and-black print W square to each end of the triangle strip to make a long border strip. Repeat to make a second long border strip.

**4.** Sew a long border strip to the long edges of the appliquéd rectangle. Press the seam allowances toward the appliquéd rectangle.

### Add the Outer Border

Sew one red-and-black print 2×12½" outer border strip to each short edge of the appliquéd rectangle. Then join one red-and-black print 2×23½" outer border strip to the long edges of the appliquéd rectangle to complete the quilt block. Press the seam allowances toward the appliquéd rectangle.

### Complete the Tray

Frame as desired. This quilt block is mounted in a frame with glass. Spacers were added between the glass and the fabric to preserve the quilt block. Attach a screw-mounted drawer pull at each end of the frame for handles.

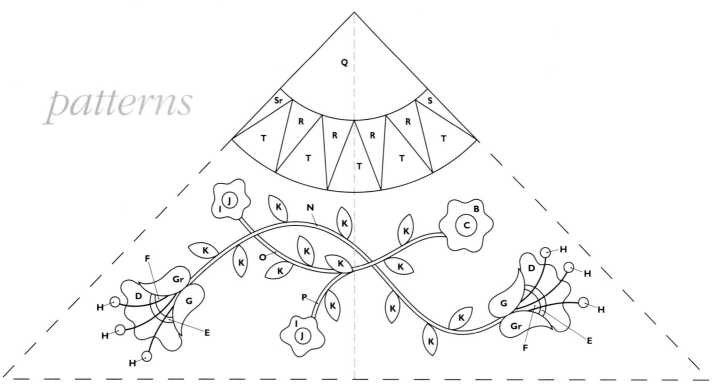

**Beauty Everlasting**
**Corner Appliqué Placement Guide**

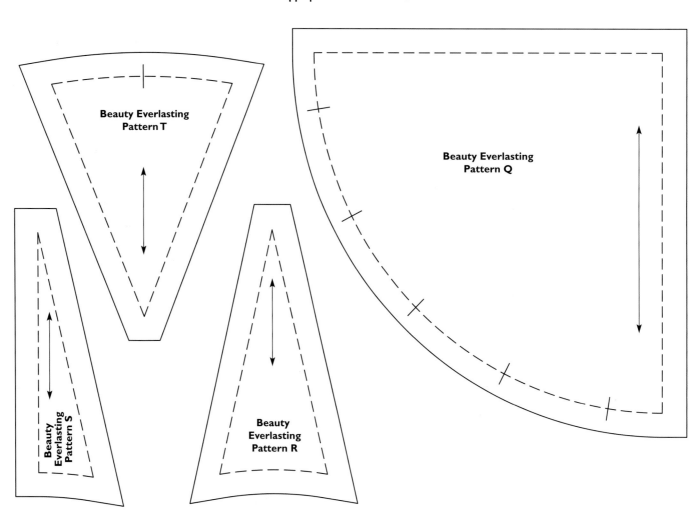

**Beauty Everlasting**
**Pattern T**

**Beauty Everlasting**
**Pattern Q**

**Beauty Everlasting Pattern S**

**Beauty Everlasting Pattern R**

The Charm of Appliqué

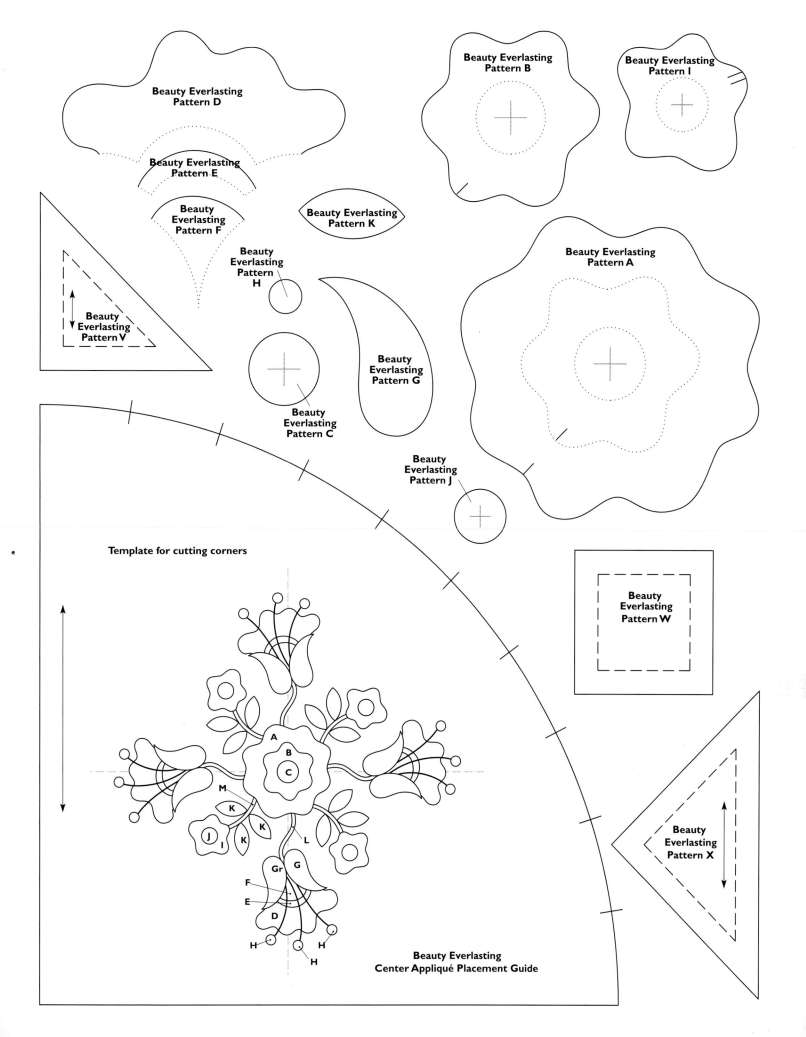

Beauty Everlasting
Pattern D

Beauty Everlasting
Pattern E

Beauty
Everlasting
Pattern F

Beauty Everlasting
Pattern B

Beauty Everlasting
Pattern I

Beauty Everlasting
Pattern K

Beauty
Everlasting
Pattern
H

Beauty Everlasting
Pattern A

Beauty
Everlasting
Pattern V

Beauty
Everlasting
Pattern C

Beauty
Everlasting
Pattern G

Beauty
Everlasting
Pattern J

Template for cutting corners

Beauty
Everlasting
Pattern W

A
B
C
M
K
K
K
J
I
L
Gr
G
F
E
D
H
H
H

Beauty
Everlasting
Pattern X

Beauty Everlasting
Center Appliqué Placement Guide

# LOVE & A LITTLE LUNACY

*This whimsical quilt, designed by Judith Hughes Marte, combines fusible-appliqué and strip piecing. You'll be dazzled when you learn how quickly you can make it. On the pages that follow you'll find two more quick projects—a scrappy pastel lap throw and an appliqué pillow.*

## the QUILT

### materials

¼ yard *each* of two light prints for blocks

½ yard total of assorted bright print scraps for appliqués and second border

⅛ yard of black print for inner border

¼ yard of red print for binding

¾ yard of backing fabric

27" square of batting

Black embroidery floss or perle cotton thread for blanket stitching (or black thread for machine appliqué)

¾ yard of fusing-adhesive material

**Finished quilt top: 25" square**
**Finished block: 4" square**

Quantities specified for 44/45"-wide, 100% cotton fabrics. All measurements include a ¼" seam allowance unless otherwise stated.

### Cut the Fabrics

To make the best use of your fabrics, cut the pieces in the order that follows. The measurements for the border strips are mathematically correct. You may wish to cut your border strips longer than specified to allow for possible sewing differences. To use fusing-adhesive material for appliquéing, as was done in this project, complete the following steps. The patterns are on *Pattern Sheet 1*.

1. Lay the fusing-adhesive material, paper side up, over the patterns. Use a pencil to trace each pattern the specified number of times, leaving ½" between tracings. Cut out the pieces roughly ¼" outside of the traced lines.

2. Following the manufacturer's instructions, press the fusing-adhesive material shapes onto the backs of the designated fabrics; let cool. Cut out the shapes on the drawn lines. Peel off the paper backing.

*continued*

From *each* of two light prints, cut:
- 10—4½" squares

From assorted bright print scraps, cut:
- 80—4½"-long strips in varying widths (Strips 1¼" to 1¾" wide were used in this quilt.)
- 5 *each* of patterns A, B, C, D, and E

From black print, cut:
- 2—1×17½" inner border strips
- 2—1×16½" inner border strips

From red print, cut:
- 3—2½×42" binding strips

## Make the Appliqué Blocks

1. Lay out 16 light print 4½" squares on a flat surface or a design wall in four rows of four squares each, with four squares reserved for the outside border (see photograph on *page 140*). Arrange the appliqué shapes on all 20 light print squares, rearranging until you're pleased with the design.

2. Fuse the shapes in place with a hot, dry iron; remember to press the Pattern E circles onto the centers of the Pattern D suns. Let the fabrics cool.

## Assemble the Quilt Top

1. Sew together the appliquéd squares in each row. Press the seam allowances in each row in one direction, alternating the direction with each row. Then join the rows to complete the quilt center. Press the seam allowances in one direction. The pieced quilt center should measure 16½" square, including the seam allowances.

2. Using two strands of black embroidery floss, blanket-stitch the appliqué pieces in place. (For specific blanket-stitching instructions, see Quilter's

Schoolhouse, which begins on *page 146*.) If your sewing machine can do a blanket stitch, you may prefer to machine-stitch around the shapes with black sewing thread.

## Add the Borders

1. Sew one black print 1×16½" inner border strip to the top and bottom edges of the pieced quilt center. Then add a black print 1×17½" inner border strip to each side edge of the pieced quilt center. Press all seam allowances toward the black print border.

2. Join the assorted scrap 4½"-long strips along their long edges to make a total of four 4½×17½"-long border units. Designer Judith Hughes Marte suggests sewing approximately 20 strips together, then trimming the unit to the correct size. Press the seam allowances in one direction.

3. Sew a border unit to the top and bottom edges of the quilt center. Press the seam allowances toward the black border. Add the remaining appliquéd squares to each end of the remaining border units. Press the seam allowances toward the appliquéd squares. Sew these units to each side edge of the pieced quilt center to complete the quilt top. Press the seam allowances toward the black borders.

## Complete the Quilt

Layer the quilt top, batting, and backing according to the instructions in Quilter's Schoolhouse, which begins on *page 146*. Quilt as desired. This quilt was machine-quilted in the ditch around each block and ¼" outside the black border. Use the red print 2½×42" strips to bind the quilt according to the instructions in Quilter's Schoolhouse.

### Love & a Little Lunacy Quilt
*optional sizes*

If you'd like to make this quilt in a size other than given, check the information *below*.

| Alternate Quilt Sizes | Crib/Lap | Twin | Full/Queen | King |
|---|---|---|---|---|
| **Number of blocks** | 68 | 220 | 382 | 604 |
| **Number of blocks wide by long** | 8×8 | 12×18 | 18×21 | 24×25 |
| **Finished size** | 41" square | 57×81" | 81×93" | 105×109" |
| | | | | |
| **Yardage requirements** | | | | |
| Each of two light prints for blocks | ⅝ yard | 1¾ yards | 2⅞ yards | 4⅜ yards |
| Bright scraps for appliqués and second border | ⅞ yard | 2½ yards | 4¼ yards | 6¾ yards |
| Black print for inner border | ⅛ yard | ¼ yard | ⅜ yard | ⅜ yard |
| Binding | ⅓ yard | ½ yard | ⅝ yard | ⅞ yard |
| Backing | 1¼ yards | 4⅞ yards | 7¼ yards | 7⅝ yards |
| Batting | 45" square | 63×87" | 87×100" | 111×115" |

# the PASTEL THROW

*Raid your fabric stash for the prettiest pastels. This scrappy quilt, inspired by the borders of "Love & a Little Lunacy," makes up in a flash.*

## materials

3 yards total of assorted pastel prints for pieced rows

6—¼-yard pieces of assorted pastel prints for sashing

⅜ yard of light yellow print for binding

1⅝ yards of backing fabric

46×59" of quilt batting

**Finished quilt top: 40×53"**

## Cut the Fabrics

To make the best use of your fabrics, cut the pieces in the order that follows.

From assorted pastel prints, cut:
- 375—4½"-long strips in varying widths
  (Strips 1¼" to 2½" wide were used in this quilt.)

From *each* of four assorted pastel prints, cut:
- 1—2½×41½" sashing strip

From *each* of two assorted pastel prints, cut:
- 1—2½×41½" sashing strip
- 1—2½×40½" sashing strip

From light yellow print, cut:
- 5—2½×42" binding strips

*continued*

## Assemble the Pieced Rows

Join the assorted pastel print 4½"-long strips along their long edges to make the following:
- 7—4½×41½" strips
- 2—4½×40½" strips

## Assemble the Quilt Top

Referring to the photograph *below* for placement, lay out the seven pieced 4½×41½" strips and the six pastel print 2½×41½" sashing strips, alternating them. Join the strips to make the pieced quilt center. Press the seam allowances toward the sashing strips. The pieced quilt center should measure 40½×41½", including the seam allowances.

## Add the Borders

1. Sew one pastel print 2½×40½" sashing strip to one pieced 4½×40½" strip to make a border unit. Press the seam allowance toward the sashing strip. Repeat with the remaining sashing strip and pieced strip to make a second border unit.

2. Join a pieced border unit to the top and bottom edges of the pieced quilt center to complete the quilt top. Press the seam allowances toward the sashing strips.

## Complete the Quilt

Layer the quilt top, batting, and backing according to the instructions in Quilter's Schoolhouse, which begins on *page 146*. Quilt as desired. This quilt was machine-quilted in an allover meandering pattern. Use the light yellow print 2½×42" strips to bind the quilt according to the instructions in Quilter's Schoolhouse.

---

# *the* PILLOW

*Four spunky appliqué blocks from the heart of the "Love & a Little Lunacy" quilt make a charming pillow.*

## materials

4—4½" squares of assorted prints for blocks

Scraps of assorted prints for appliqués

¼ yard of solid black for borders and binding

⅔ yard of dark brown print for border and back

21" square of quilt batting

21" square of muslin for lining

14" pillow form

Scraps of fusing-adhesive material

**Finished pillow top: 14" square**

## Cut the Fabrics

To make the best use of your fabrics, cut the pieces in the order that follows. For this project, we used fusing-adhesive material for appliquéing. To use this same method, follow the Cut the Fabrics instructions, steps 1 and 2, on *page 141*. This project uses "Love & a Little Lunacy" patterns, which are on *Pattern Sheet 1*.

From scraps of assorted prints, cut:
- 1 *each* of patterns A, B, C, D, and E

From solid black, cut:
- 2—2½×42" binding strips
- 2—1½×10½" inner border strips
- 2—1½×8½" inner border strips
- 4—2½" squares

From dark brown prints, cut:
- 2—19×14½" rectangles for pillow back
- 4—2½×10½" outer border strips

## Assemble the Pillow Center

1. Fuse the appliqué shapes in place on the assorted print 4½" squares with a hot, dry iron. Let the fabrics cool.

2. Sew together the four appliquéd squares in two rows. Press the seam allowances in each row in opposite directions. Then join the rows to make the pillow center. Press the seam allowance in one direction.

3. Using black thread, blanket-stitch the appliqué pieces in place.

## Add the Borders

1. Sew a solid black 1½×8½" inner border strip to the top and bottom edges of the pieced pillow center. Join a solid black 1½×10½" inner border strip to each side edge of the pieced pillow center. Press all seam allowances toward the black border.

2. Sew a brown print 2½×10½" outer border strip to the top and bottom edges of the pieced pillow center. Press the seam allowances toward the outer border. Add a solid black 2½" square to each end of the remaining brown print outer

border strips. Press the seam allowances toward the solid black squares. Sew these border strips to each side edge of the pieced pillow center to complete the pillow top. Press the seam allowances toward the outer border.

## Complete the Pillow

1. Layer the pillow top, batting, and muslin lining as instructed in Quilter's Schoolhouse, which begins on *page 146*. Quilt as desired. This pillow top was machine-quilted in the ditch around each block and border piece; a moon, star, heart, or flower was stitched in each border square.

2. With wrong sides inside, fold each dark brown print 19×14½" rectangle in half to form two double-thick 9½×14½" pieces. Overlap the folded edges by 2". Stitch across the folds, ½" from the top and bottom edges, to secure the pieces, creating the pillow back. The two layers make the pillow back more stable and finish it nicely.

3. With wrong sides together, layer the pillow top and the pillow back. Sew the pieces together along all four edges; turn right side out.

4. Bind the pillow top with the solid black 2½×42" strips according to the instructions in Quilter's Schoolhouse, which begins on *page 146*. Insert the pillow form through the back opening.

# GETTING STARTED

*Before you begin any quilting project, it's wise to collect the tools and materials you'll need in one place. If you're an experienced sewer, you'll find you own some of the necessary equipment. Items that have been adapted specifically for quilters are available in fabric and quilt stores.*

## Gather Your Tools

### CUTTING

• **Acrylic ruler:** For making perfectly straight cuts with a rotary cutter, choose a ruler of thick, clear plastic. Many sizes are available. A 6×12" ruler marked in ¼" increments with 30°, 45°, and 60° angles is a good first purchase.

• **Rotary cutter and mat:** These tools have revolutionized quilting because a rotary cutter's round blade cuts strips, squares, triangles, and diamonds more quickly, efficiently, and accurately than scissors. A rotary cutter should always be used with a mat designed specifically for it. In addition to protecting your work surface, the mat helps keep the fabric from shifting while you cut.

• **Scissors:** You'll need one pair for fabric and another for paper and plastic.

• **Pencils and other marking tools:** Marks made with special quilt markers are easy to remove after sewing and quilting.

• **Template plastic:** This slightly frosted plastic comes in sheets about ¹⁄₁₆" thick.

### PIECING

• **Iron and ironing board:** Pressing the seams ensures accurate piecing.

• **Sewing thread:** Use 100-percent-

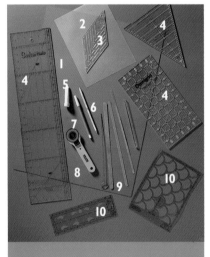

### Basic Tools

1. Rotary cutting mat
2. Template plastic
3. Template
4. Acrylic rulers
5. Chalk marker
6. Marking pencil
7. Water-erasable marker
8. Rotary cutter
9. Bias bars
10. Quilting stencils

cotton or a cotton-covered polyester thread.

• **Sewing machine:** Any machine with well-adjusted tension will produce pucker-free patchwork seams.

### APPLIQUÉ

• **Fusing-adhesive material:** Instead of the traditional pinning method, secure cutout shapes to the background of an appliqué block with this iron-on adhesive.

• **Hand-sewing needles:** For hand appliqué, most quilters like fine quilting needles.

### HAND QUILTING

• **Frame or hoop:** You'll get smaller, more even stitches if you stretch your quilt as you stitch. A frame supports the quilt's weight, ensures even tension, and frees both hands for stitching. However, once set up, it cannot be disassembled until the quilting is complete. Hoops are more portable and less expensive. Quilting hoops are deeper than embroidery hoops to handle the thickness of quilt layers.

• **Quilting needles:** A "between" or quilting needle is short with a small eye. Common sizes are 8, 9, and 10; size 8 is best for beginners.

• **Quilting thread:** Quilting thread, including the preferred 100-percent-cotton variety, is stronger than sewing thread.

• **Thimble:** This finger cover relieves the pressure required to push a needle through several layers of fabric and batting.

## MACHINE QUILTING

- **Darning foot:** You may find this tool, also called a hopper foot, in your sewing machine's accessory kit. If not, have the model and brand of your machine available when you go to purchase one. It's used for free-motion stitching.
- **Safety pins:** They hold the layers together during·quilting.
- **Table or other large work surface that's level with your machine bed:** Your quilt will need the support.
- **Thread:** Choose from 100-percent-cotton quilting thread, cotton-wrapped polyester quilting thread, and very fine nylon monofilament thread.
- **Walking foot:** This sewing-machine accessory helps keep long straight quilting lines smooth.

### Select a First Project

For beginners and pros alike, choosing a project is the first step in successful quilting. There are so many fabrics, patterns, and ideas, picking a first project can be confusing. Here are some tips.

**Find a friendly place:** A quilt shop or other store where the employees are knowledgeable about quilting is the best place to start. Chances are, the employees will relish initiating a new quilter.

**Start small:** A wall hanging or pillow takes less time to complete.

**Take a class:** Most quilting shops offer classes, making it easy to solve a problem when it arises.

**Buy a kit:** If selecting four or five fabrics from the hundreds of bolts in the store overwhelms you, a kit that includes all the fabrics may be the answer.

**Be square:** Pieced projects made up of squares, rectangles, and right triangles are among the easiest. Or look for an appliqué project with simple shapes or one that uses fusible-adhesive material.

**Love it:** Encourage yourself to finish by choosing a design that you're eager to finish and display or give as a gift.

### Choose Your Fabrics

It is not just an old wive's tale that 100-percent cotton is the best fabric for quiltmaking. Cotton fabric minimizes seam distortion, presses crisply, and is easy to quilt. Most patterns, including those in this book, specify quantities for 44/45"-wide fabrics unless otherwise noted. Our projects call for a little extra yardage in length to allow for minor errors and slight shrinkage.

### Prepare Your Fabrics

There are conflicting opinions about the need to prewash fabric. The debate is a modern one because most antique quilts were made with unwashed fabric. However, the dyes and sizing used today are unlike those used a century ago.

Prewashing fabric offers quilters certainty as its main advantage. Today's fabrics resist bleeding and shrinking, but some of both can occur in some fabrics—an unpleasant prospect once you've assembled the quilt. Some quilters find prewashed fabric easier to quilt. If you choose to prewash your fabric, you'll need to press it well before cutting.

Other quilters prefer the crispness of unwashed fabric for machine piecing. And, if you use fabrics with the same fiber content throughout the quilt, then any shrinkage that occurs in its first washing should be uniform. Other quilters find this small amount of shrinkage desirable, since it gives the quilt a slightly puckered, antique look.

We recommend that you prewash a scrap of each fabric to test it for shrinkage and bleeding. If you choose to prewash a fabric, unfold it to a single layer. Wash it in warm water to allow the fabric to shrink and/or bleed. If the fabric bleeds, rinse it until the water runs clear. Do not use any fabric in your quilt if it has not stopped bleeding. Hang the fabric to dry, or tumble it in the dryer until just slightly damp. Press the fabric before marking and cutting.

### Select the Batting

For a small beginner project, a thin cotton batting is a good choice. It has a tendency to "stick" to fabric so it requires less basting. Also, it's easy to stitch. It's wise to follow the stitch density (distance between rows of stitching required to keep the batting from shifting and wadding up inside the quilt) recommendation printed on the packaging. Cotton batting is a good choice for garments because it shapes to the body.

Polyester batting is lightweight and readily available. In general, it springs back to its original height when compressed, adding a puffiness to quilts. It tends to "beard" (work out between the weave of the fabric) more than natural fibers. Polyester fleece is denser and works well for pillow tops and place mats.

Wool batting has better loft retention and absorbs moisture, making it ideal for cool, damp climates. Read the label carefully before purchasing a wool batting because it may require special handling.

# CUTTING WITH TEMPLATES

*A successful quilt requires precise cutting of pieces. The traditional method employs scissors and patterns called templates. It's the best way to cut curved pieces, and many quilters enjoy it for other shapes too. Or, you can speed-cut squares, rectangles, and triangles using the rotary techniques described on pages 150 and 151.*

## About Scissors

Sharp scissor blades are vital to accurate cutting, but keeping them sharp is difficult because each use dulls the metal slightly. Cutting paper and plastic speeds the dulling process, so invest in a second pair for those materials and reserve your best scissors for fabric.

## Make the Templates

For some quilts, you'll need to cut out the same shape up to 200 or more times. For accurate piecing later, the individual pieces should be identical to one another. The secret is in the templates.

A template is a pattern made from extra-sturdy material so you can trace around it many times without wearing away the edges. Acrylic templates for many common shapes are available at quilt shops. Or, you can make your own by duplicating printed patterns (like those in the Pattern Packet) on plastic.

To make permanent templates, we recommend using easy-to-cut template plastic, available at crafts supply stores. This material lasts indefinitely, and its transparency allows you to trace a pattern directly onto its surface.

To make a template, lay the plastic over a printed pattern. Trace the pattern onto the plastic using a ruler and a permanent marker. This will ensure straight lines, accurate corners, and permanency.

For hand piecing and appliqué, make templates the exact size of the finished pieces, without seam allowances, by tracing the patterns' dashed lines. For machine piecing, make templates with seam allowances included.

For easy reference, mark each template with its letter designation, grain line if noted, and block name. Verify the template's size by placing it over the printed pattern. Templates must be accurate or the error, however small, will compound many times as you assemble the quilt. To check the accuracy of your templates, make a test block before cutting the fabric pieces for an entire quilt.

## Trace the Templates

To mark on fabric, use a pencil, white dressmaker's pencil, chalk, or a special quilt marker that makes a thin, accurate line. Do not use a ballpoint or ink pen that may bleed if washed. Test all marking tools on a fabric scrap before using them.

To trace pieces that will be used for hand piecing or appliqué, place templates facedown on the wrong side of the fabric and trace; position the tracings at least ½" apart (see Diagram 1, Template A). The lines drawn on the fabric are the sewing lines. Mark cutting lines, or estimate by eye a seam allowance around each piece as you cut out the pieces. For hand piecing, add a ¼" seam allowance when cutting out the pieces; for hand appliqué, add a 3⁄16" seam allowance.

Templates used to make pieces for

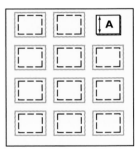

**Diagram 1**

machine piecing have seam allowances included so you can use common lines for efficient cutting. Place the templates facedown on the wrong side of the fabric and trace; position them without space in between (see Diagram 2, Template B). Using sharp scissors or a rotary cutter and ruler, cut precisely on the drawn (cutting) lines.

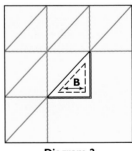

**Diagram 2**

## Templates for Angled Pieces

When two patchwork pieces come together and form an angled opening, a third piece must be set into this angle. This happens frequently when using diamond shapes.

For a design that requires setting in, a pinhole or window template makes it easy to mark the fabric with each shape's exact sewing and cutting lines and the exact point of each corner on the sewing line. By matching the corners of adjacent pieces, you'll be able to sew them together easily and accurately.

To make a pinhole template, lay template plastic over a pattern piece. Trace both the cutting and sewing lines onto the plastic. Carefully cut out the template on the cutting line. Using a sewing-machine needle or any large needle, make a hole in the template at each corner on the sewing line (matching points). The holes must be large enough for a pencil point or other fabric marker to poke through.

To make a window template, lay the template plastic over a pattern piece. Trace both the cutting and sewing lines onto the plastic. Cut out the template on the cutting line. Then, with a crafts knife, cut on the sewing line, and remove the center of the template.

### Trace Angled Pieces

To mark fabric using a pinhole template, lay it facedown on the wrong side of the fabric and trace. Using a pencil, mark dots on the fabric through the holes in the template to create matching points. Cut out the fabric piece on the drawn line, making sure the matching points are marked.

To mark fabric using a window template, lay it facedown on the wrong side of the fabric (see Diagram 3). With a marking tool,

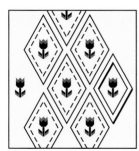

**Diagram 3**

mark the cutting line, sewing line, and each corner on the sewing line (matching points). Cut out the fabric piece on the cutting lines, making sure all pieces have sewing lines and matching points marked.

### Cut Bias Strips

Strips for curved appliqué pattern pieces, such as meandering vines, and for binding curved edges should be cut on the bias (diagonally across the grain of a woven fabric), which runs at a 45° angle to the selvage and has the most give or stretch.

To cut bias strips, begin with a fabric square or rectangle. Use a large acrylic ruler to square up the left edge of the fabric. Make the first cut at a 45° angle to the left edge (Diagram 4). Handle the diagonal edges carefully to avoid distorting the bias. To cut a strip, measure the desired width parallel to the 45° cut edge; cut. Continue cutting enough strips to total the length needed.

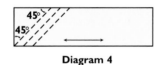

**Diagram 4**

### Consider the Grain

*American Patchwork & Quilting®* instructions list pieces in the order they should be cut to make the best use of your fabric. Always consider the fabric grain before cutting. The arrow on a pattern piece indicates which direction the fabric grain should run. One or more straight sides of the pattern piece should follow the fabric's lengthwise or crosswise grain. The lengthwise grain, parallel to the selvage (the tightly finished edge), has the least amount of stretch. (Do not use the selvage of a woven fabric in a quilt. When washed, it may shrink more than the rest of the fabric.) Crosswise grain, perpendicular to the selvage, has a little more give. The edge of any pattern piece that will be on the outside of a block or a quilt should always be cut on the lengthwise grain.

In projects larger than 42" in length or width, most of our patterns specify that the border strips be cut the width (crosswise grain) of the fabric and pieced to use the least amount of fabric. If you'd prefer to cut the border strips on the lengthwise grain and not piece them, you'll need to refigure the yardage to accommodate this.

### Continuous Binding

Quilts with simple straight edges can be bound using straight-grain binding. You can get straight-grain binding by piecing cut strips end to end or by using the continuous-cut method.

For continuous cutting, start with a square or rectangle of fabric. Draw a diagonal line as if you were preparing to cut bias strips. Cut on the drawn line.

Sew the resulting two pieces together with a ¼" seam allowance, as shown in Diagram 5. Press the seam open. Use a quilt marker and a ruler to draw parallel lines across the length of the seamed fabric piece. The space between the lines is the desired width of the binding strip, including seam allowances. For example, space the lines 2" apart for a ⅜"-wide finished binding.

Bring the bias edges together, matching right sides, to create a tube. Offset the edges by shifting one down so that the top of one edge aligns with the first marked line of the opposite edge (Diagram 6). Holding the fabric in this position, sew the bias edges together. Press the seam open.

Begin cutting on the top marked line and cut in a continuous spiral (Diagram 7). Each time you cut across the seam, you'll be moving down one marked line.

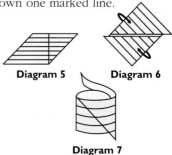

**Diagram 5**   **Diagram 6**

**Diagram 7**

# ROTARY CUTTING

*Specialized products for rotary cutting not only save time and labor, they also eliminate the need for patterns and templates in basic shapes, such as squares and triangles. A rotary cutter, a self-healing protective mat, and a thick acrylic ruler allow you to make quick and efficient straight cuts.*

## About the Tools

The round blade of a rotary cutter will cut up to six layers of fabric at once. Because the blade is so sharp, be sure to purchase one with a safety guard and keep the guard over the blade when you're not cutting.

Hold the rotary cutter at a 45° angle to the cutting surface. When cutting fabric, keep an even pressure on the rotary cutter. The less you move your fabric when cutting, the more accurate your cutting will be.

If you haven't cut through all the fabric layers, check the following:
• Is the blade dull?
• Is there a nick in the blade?
• Did you put enough pressure on the rotary cutter?

## Cutting Squares

To cut four 9½" squares, follow these rotary-cutting instructions.

**1.** Iron the fabric. Find its crosswise grain. Lay the fabric on the rotary mat with the right side down and one selvage away from you. Fold the fabric with the wrong side inside and the selvages together. Fold the fabric in half again, lining up the fold with the selvage edges (see Photograph 1). Lightly hand-crease all of the folds.

**2.** Trim the raw edge of the fabric. To ensure straight cuts, align the 1" mark on the bottom of the ruler with the bottom fold of the fabric

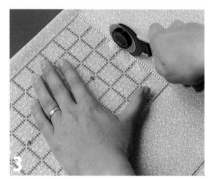

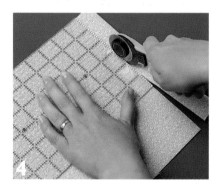

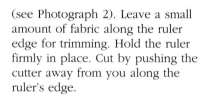

(see Photograph 2). Leave a small amount of fabric along the ruler edge for trimming. Hold the ruler firmly in place. Cut by pushing the cutter away from you along the ruler's edge.

**3.** Turn your cutting mat clockwise 90° with the newly cut edge toward you. Find the 9½" mark on the ruler, then line up the 9½" mark with the bottom edge of the fabric. Be sure to leave a small amount of fabric to trim. With one hand, hold the ruler firmly in place. Use your other hand to cut the fabric the length of the ruler. Without moving the ruler, turn the corner and continue to cut along the ruler's short edge.

**4.** Turn your cutting mat clockwise 90° with the newly cut edge toward you. Keeping the 9½" mark on the ruler lined up with the same straight edge, slide the ruler toward the folded edge of fabric. Continue cutting along the ruler's short edge to finish cutting the fabric (see Photograph 3). You now should have three squared sides.

**5.** Again, turn your cutting mat clockwise 90° with the newly cut edge toward you (the side remaining to be cut should be on the right). Line up the 9½" mark on the ruler with the left straight edge. Begin cutting the right edge. Finally,

slide the ruler up to finish cutting the edge (see Photograph 4 *opposite*). You now should have four 9½" squares.

Quilting instructions frequently say:
**From assorted dark scraps, cut:**
• 30—3¼" squares, cutting each diagonally twice in an X for a total of 120 triangles.

To make the triangles, follow these rotary-cutting instructions.

**1.** Square up the fabric by trimming the raw edge of the fabric as directed in steps 1 and 2, *opposite*.

**2.** Turn your cutting mat clockwise 180° with the newly cut edge on the left. Find the 3¼" mark on the ruler. Line up the 3¼" mark with the left straight of the fabric (see Photograph 5). Line up the 1" mark with the bottom fold of fabric. Cut along ruler edge. You now should have one 3¼"-wide strip.

**3.** Unfold the strip. Turn it so a narrow end is on the left. Line up

the 3¼" mark on the ruler with the left edge of the fabric, and cut along the ruler's right edge. You now should have a 3¼" square. Repeat to cut a specified number of squares.

**4.** To cut each square diagonally twice in an X, line up the ruler's edge with opposite corners (see Photograph 6). Cut along the ruler's edge; do not separate the two triangles created. Line up the ruler's edge with the remaining corners and cut (see Photograph 7).

---

# TIMESAVERS

Many quilts employ a strip-piecing technique that takes further advantage of rotary cutting. To illustrate how it works, here are three practice squares. Each makes a 6" finished square.

**Easy Triangle-Squares**
When a pattern calls for many triangle-squares of the same two fabrics, cut 6⅞" strips, pair the strips with right sides together, and cut the layered strips into 6⅞" squares. Place a layered pair of squares on a piece of 220-grit sandpaper. Use a pencil and ruler to draw a diagonal line on the top square. Stitch ¼" on each side of the drawn line (see diagrams *right*). Save more time by chain-piecing (see *page 152*). Rotary-cut each pair of squares apart on the drawn line.

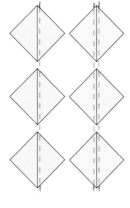

**Four-Patch Magic**
For a 6" Four-Patch square, cut a 3½×42" strip from two different fabrics and sew them together lengthwise; press. Use a ruler and rotary cutter to cut two 3½"-wide segments (see diagrams *below*). Rotate one of the segments 180°, match seam lines, and sew together.

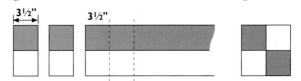

**Nine-Patch Now**
For a 6" Nine-Patch square, cut three 2½×42" strips from each of two fabrics. Sew the strips together lengthwise into strip sets of three, alternating fabrics (see diagrams *below left*); press. Use the rotary cutter and ruler to cut two 2½"-wide segments from the first strip set and one 2½"-wide segment from the second strip set. Sew the three segments together as shown in the diagram *below right*.

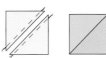

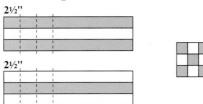

# PIECING

*Patchwork piecing consists of sewing fabric pieces together in a specific pattern. There are several approaches to piecing a quilt. Understanding each one helps you choose the one you'll enjoy most.*

## Hand Piecing

In hand piecing, seams are sewn only on the marked sewing lines rather than from one raw edge to the other. Begin by matching the edges of two pieces with the right sides of the fabrics together. Sewing lines should be marked on the wrong side of both pieces. Push a pin through both fabric layers at each corner (see Diagram 1). Secure the pins perpendicular to the sewing line. Insert more pins between the corners.

**Diagram 1**          **Diagram 2**

Insert a needle through both fabrics at the seam-line corner. Make one or two backstitches atop the first stitch to secure the thread. Weave the needle in and out of the fabric along the seam line, taking four to six tiny stitches at a time before you pull the thread taut (see Diagram 2). Remove the pins as you sew. Turn the work over occasionally to see that the stitching follows the marked sewing line on the other side.

Sew eight to 10 stitches per inch along the seam line. At the end of the seam, remove the last pin and make the ending stitch through the hole left by the corner pin. Backstitch over the last stitch and end the seam with a loop knot (see Diagram 3).

**Diagram 3**

To join rows of patchwork by hand, hold the sewn pieces with right sides together and seams matching. Insert pins at corners of the matching pieces. Add additional pins as necessary, securing each pin perpendicular to the sewing line (see Diagram 4).

Stitch the joining seam as before,

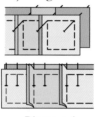

**Diagram 4**

but do not sew across the seam allowances that join the patches. At each seam allowance, make a backstitch or loop knot, then slide the needle through the seam allowance. (see Diagram 5). Knot or backstitch again to give the intersection strength, then sew the remainder of the seam. Press each seam as it is completed.

**Diagram 5**

## Machine Piecing

Machine piecing depends on sewing an exact ¼" seam allowance. Some machines have a presser foot that is the proper width or a ¼" foot is available. To check the width of a machine's presser foot, sew a sample seam, with the raw fabric edges aligned with the right edge of the presser foot; measure the resultant seam allowance using graph paper with a ¼" grid.

If the presser foot does not indicate ¼", mark the distance on the throat plate with the aid of graph paper. Carefully trim graph paper along a grid line. Place the trimmed graph paper under the needle. Slowly lower the needle into the grid one

line from the newly trimmed edge (see Diagram 6). Use masking tape to mark the new seam guide's location ahead of the needle.

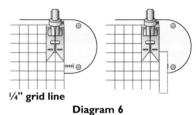

**¼" grid line**

**Diagram 6**

To test your newly marked seam guide, cut three 1½"-wide strips of different fabric scraps. Sew together two of the strips. Join the third strip. Press the seam allowances away from the center. If your seam is ¼" wide, the center strip should measure 1" (see Diagram 7). If not, adjust your seam guide.

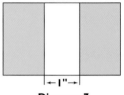

**←1"→**

**Diagram 7**

## Choosing Thread Color

Using two different thread colors—one on top of the machine and one in the bobbin—can help you to better match your thread color to your fabrics. If your quilt has many fabrics, use a neutral color, such as gray or beige, for both the top and bobbin threads throughout the quilt.

## Chain Piecing

In machine piecing, squares and triangles in blocks should be sewn together from edge to edge. Save time and thread by chain-piecing whenever possible. To chain-piece, feed the pieces under the machine needle without lifting the foot or clipping the thread. The stitched patches will be linked by short lengths of thread; clip the threads to cut them apart.

In quilting, almost every seam needs to be pressed before the piece is sewn to another, so keep your iron and ironing board near your sewing area. It's important to remember to press with an up and down motion. Moving the iron around on the fabric can distort seams, especially those sewn on the bias.

Project instructions in this book generally tell you in what direction to press each seam. When in doubt, press both seam allowances toward the darker fabric. When joining rows of blocks, alternate the direction the seam allowances are pressed to ensure flat corners.

## Setting in Pieces

The key to sewing angled pieces together is aligning marked matching points carefully. Whether you're stitching by machine or hand, start and stop sewing precisely at the matching points (see the dots in Diagram 8, top) and backstitch to secure the ends of the seams. This prepares the angle for the next piece to be set in.

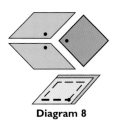

**Diagram 8**

Join two diamond pieces, sewing between matching points to make an angled unit (see Diagram 8, bottom).

Follow the specific instructions for either machine or hand piecing to complete the set-in seam.

MACHINE PIECING
With right sides together, pin one piece of the angled unit to one edge of the square (see Diagram 9). Match the seam's matching points, by pushing a pin through both fabric layers to check the alignment. Machine-stitch the seam between

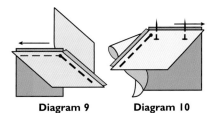

**Diagram 9**    **Diagram 10**

the matching points. Backstitch to secure the ends of the seam; do not stitch into the ¼" seam allowance. Remove the unit from the sewing machine.

Bring the adjacent edge of the angled unit up and align it with the next edge of the square (see Diagram 10). Insert a pin in each corner to align matching points, then pin the remainder of the seam. Machine-stitch between matching points as before. Press the seam allowances of the set-in piece away from it.

HAND PIECING
Pin one piece of the angled unit to one edge of the square with right sides together (see Diagram 11). Use pins to align matching points at the corners.

Hand-sew the seam from the open end of the angle into the corner. Remove pins as you sew between matching points. Backstitch at the corner to secure stitches. Do not sew into the ¼" seam allowance and do not cut your thread.

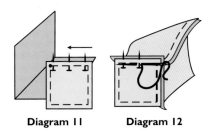

**Diagram 11**    **Diagram 12**

Bring the adjacent edge of the square up and align it with the other edge of the angled unit. Insert a pin in each corner to align matching points, then pin the remainder of the seam (see Diagram 12). Hand-sew the seam from the corner to the open end of the angle, removing pins as you sew. Press the seam allowances of the set-in piece away from it.

## Mitered Border Corners

A border surrounds the piecework of many quilts. Angled, mitered corners add to a border's framed effect.

To add a border with mitered corners, first pin a border strip to a quilt top edge, matching the center of the strip and the center of the quilt top edge. Sew together, beginning and ending the seam ¼" from the quilt top corners (see Diagram 13). Allow excess border fabric to extend beyond the edges. Repeat with remaining border strips. Press the seam allowances toward the border strips.

**Diagram 13**

Overlap the border strips at each corner (see Diagram 14). Align the edge of a 90° right triangle with the raw edge of a top border strip so the long edge of the triangle intersects the seam in the corner. With a pencil, draw along the edge of the triangle from the border seam out to the raw edge. Place the bottom border strip on top and repeat the marking process.

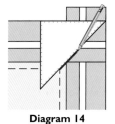

**Diagram 14**

With the right sides of adjacent border strips together, match the marked seam lines and pin (see Diagram 15).

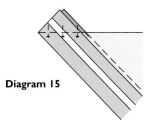

**Diagram 15**

Beginning with a backstitch at the inside corner, stitch exactly on the marked lines to the outside edges of the border strips. Check the right side of the corner to see that it lies flat. Then trim the excess fabric, leaving a ¼" seam allowance. Press the seam open. Mark and sew the remaining corners in this manner.

# APPLIQUÉ

*With appliqué, you create a picture by stitching fabric shapes atop
a foundation block. Traditionally, the edges of each shape are turned under.
Then the shapes are hand-sewn to the foundation fabric with hidden slip
stitches or with embroidery stitches, such as the blanket stitch.
We're offering some shortcuts for today's busy quilters.*

### Start Simple

We encourage beginners to select an appliqué design with straight lines and gentle curves. Learning to make sharp points and tiny stitches takes practice.

In the following instructions, we've used a stemmed flower motif as the appliqué example.

### Baste the Seam Allowances

Begin by turning under the appliqué piece ³⁄₁₆" seam allowances; press. Some quilters like to thread-baste the folded edges to ensure proper placement. Edges that will be covered by other pieces don't need to be turned under.

For sharp points on tips, trim the seam allowance to within ⅛" of the stitching line (see Photograph 1); taper the sides gradually to ³⁄₁₆". Fold under the seam allowance remaining on the tips. Then turn the seam allowances under on both sides of the tips. The side seam allowances will overlap slightly at the tips, forming sharp points. Baste the folded edges in place (see Photograph 2). The turned seam allowances may form little pleats on the back side that you also should baste in place. You'll remove the basting stitches after the shape has been appliquéd to the foundation.

### Make Bias Stems

In order to curve gracefully, appliqué stems are cut on the bias. The strips for stems can be prepared in two ways. You can fold and press the strip in thirds as shown in Photograph 3. Or you can fold the

bias strip in half lengthwise with the wrong side inside; press. Stitch ¼" in from the raw edges to keep them aligned. Fold the strip in half again, hiding the raw edges behind the first folded edge; press.

### Position and Stitch

Pin the prepared appliqué pieces in place on the foundation using the position markings or referring to the block assembly diagram (see Photograph 4). If your pattern suggests it, mark the position for each piece on the foundation block

before you begin. Overlap the flowers and stems as indicated.

Using thread in colors that match the fabrics, sew each stem and blossom onto the foundation with small slip stitches as shown in Photograph 5. (For photographic purposes, the thread color does not match the lily.)

Catch only a few threads of the stem or flower fold with each stitch. Pull the stitches taut but not so tight that they pucker the fabric. You can use the needle's point to manipulate the appliqué edges as needed. Take an extra slip stitch at the point of a petal to secure it to the foundation.

You can use hand-quilting needles for appliqué stitching, but some quilters prefer a longer milliners or straw needle. The extra length of the needle aids in tucking fabric under before taking slip stitches.

If the foundation fabric shows through the appliqué fabrics, cut away the foundation fabric. Trimming the foundation fabric also reduces the bulk of multiple layers when quilting. Carefully trim the underlying fabric to within ¼" of the appliqué stitches (see Photograph 6 *opposite*). Do not cut the appliqué fabric.

(see Photograph 6 *opposite*)

### Double Appliqué

To ease the challenge of turning curved edges, many quilters prefer to face appliqué pieces. For this, trace each template onto the wrong side of the fabric. Cut out, leaving a ¼" seam allowance around all of the edges.

Place the cut piece, right side down, on a piece of sheer, nonfusible, nonwoven interfacing. Sew all the way around on the drawn line. Trim the interfacing slightly smaller than the fabric and clip inner curves.

Make a small clip in the center of the interfacing (see Diagram 1). Turn the appliqué right side out through the clipped opening. Press the piece from the fabric side, making sure no interfacing shows at the edges.

**Diagram 1**

### Fusible Appliqué

For quick-finish appliqué, use paper-backed fusing-adhesive material. Then you can iron the shapes onto the foundation and add decorative stitching to the edges. This product consists of two layers, a fusible webbing lightly bonded to paper that peels off. The webbing adds a slight stiffness to the back of the appliqué pieces.

When you purchase this product, read the directions on the bolt end or packaging to make sure you're buying the right kind for your project. Some brands are specifically engineered to bond fabrics with no sewing at all. If you try to stitch fabric after it has bonded with one of these products, you may encounter difficulty. Some paper-backed fusible products are made exclusively for sewn edges; others work with or without stitching.

If you buy paper-backed fusing-adhesive material from a bolt, be sure fusing instructions are included because the iron temperature and timing varies by brand. This information is usually on the paper backing.

With any of these products, the general procedure is to trace the pattern wrong side up onto the paper side of the fusing-adhesive material. Then place the fusing-adhesive material on the wrong side of the appliqué fabrics, paper side up, and use an iron to fuse the layers together. Then cut out the shapes, peel off the paper, turn the fabrics right side up, and fuse the shapes to the foundation fabric.

You also can fuse the fusing-adhesive material and fabric together before tracing. You'll still need to trace templates wrong side up on the paper backing.

If you've used a no-sew fusing-adhesive material, your appliqué is done. There also are several appealing ways to finish the edges of appliqué with stitching.

### Blanket Stitch

This book's patterns often specify hand-worked blanket stitches (see Photograph 7).

Using embroidery floss in a color that coordinates with the fabric color, pull the needle up at A, form

a reverse L shape with the floss, and hold the angle of the L shape in place with your thumb. Push the needle down at B and come up at C to secure the stitch. Repeat the steps until you've stitched around the piece (see Diagram 2).

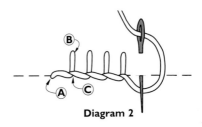

**Diagram 2**

### Machine Stitches

The sewing machine offers several other decorative options. To simply secure the edges, standard zigzag stitches provide a neat finish. Using matching or contrasting thread produces distinctly different looks. For invisibility, use a hem stitch that consists of three or four straight stitches followed by a V stitch. Keep the straight stitches on the foundation and catch the appliquéd shape with the V. To dramatize appliquéd shapes, try satin (see Photograph 8 *below*) or other decorative stitches worked in a contrasting thread.

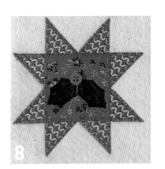

# QUILTING

*A quilt top becomes a finished quilt when stitched to batting and backing. The layers can be secured by hand, machine, or tying. Choose a method that harmonizes with your quilt's design and intended use.*

## Choose a Quilting Design

After you decide whether to hand- or machine-stitch, you still have decisions to make about the design you'll stitch in the quilt top.

**Background fillers** are simple designs in the open spaces. Most background fillers are patterns of straight lines, such as single or closely spaced double lines stitched vertically, horizontally, or diagonally. Crossed stitching lines make square or diamond grids.

**Freestyle designs** are meandering, allover patterns. Machine quilters refer to the technique as stippling.

**Echo quilting** is multiple lines of stitching that follow the outline of an appliqué or other design element, echoing its shape.

**Quilting in the ditch** is stitching close to the seam line on the side that does not have seam allowances. These stitches are more subtle than outline quilting (see photograph *right*) because they tend to disappear into seam lines.

**Outline quilting** stitches are made ¼" from the seam lines, just past the extra thickness of the pressed seam.

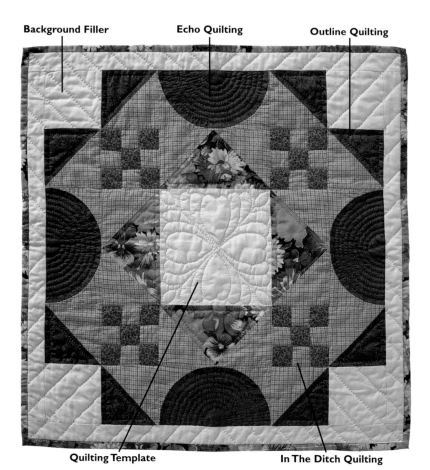

Background Filler     Echo Quilting     Outline Quilting

Quilting Template     In The Ditch Quilting

## Mark the Design

Freestyle, outline, and in-the-ditch quilting do not require marking on the quilt top. For other designs, you'll need to mark the top, tracing a stencil, template, or drawing.

Before you begin, press the quilt top. Be sure to test your marker to make sure it shows up on the fabric and is easy to remove when finished.

Secure the template on a flat surface with masking tape. Match the quilt top seams with the edge guides of the pattern (Photograph

**1**

1). Firmly secure the quilt top over the template with masking tape.

Begin marking at the center of the quilt top and work toward the borders (Photograph 2). Mark the

**2**

larger and/or more complex designs first, then fill in the smaller details. Mark the background filler last, if you choose to stitch one. Use a ruler to draw straight lines.

## Baste the Layers

Properly assembling a quilt's layers ensures a smooth, wrinkle-free surface for quilting. Cut or piece the backing fabric so it is at least 3" larger on all sides than the quilt top. Fluff precut batting in a clothes dryer for a few minutes on an air-dry setting to remove wrinkles. Trim the batting so it is 3" larger all around than the quilt top.

Tape the backing to a smooth work surface, wrong side up. Center the batting atop the backing, smoothing it flat; tape or pin them together at the edges. Center the quilt top on the batting.

Baste the three layers together by stitching a horizontal and vertical line through the center to form quadrants on the quilt top. The basting stitches should be about 2" long and 4" apart (Photograph 3). If you will be lap-quilting, make the basting stitches closer together since the quilt will be handled more. If you will be machine-quilting, you may substitute No. 1 safety pins for basting, pinning through all layers in the same pattern.

## Hand Quilting

Viewed as the traditional method, hand quilting can take more time than piecing the top. Some stitchers like to hold the quilt loosely in their laps. Most feel, however, that straighter, smaller stitches are achieved if the work is held taut in a hoop or frame.

Stitch with about 18" of thread in your needle; knot one end. No knots should show on the front or back of a hand-quilted piece. To bury a knot inside the quilt, insert

the needle through the top and the batting (but not the backing), a few inches away from the quilting area. Bring the needle back to the surface in position to make the first stitch. Gently tug on the thread, just enough to pop the knot through the top fabric and embed it in the batting.

To end stitching, wind the thread twice around the needle close to the top, making a French knot. Then run the needle through the top and batting, bring it out a few inches away from the stitching. Hold the thread taut, clip it close to the top, and release it; the thread end will snap out of sight.

## Quilting Stitches

Hand quilting takes practice. To begin, hold the needle between your thumb and index finger. Place your other hand under the quilt, with the tip of your index finger on the spot where the needle will come through the quilt back. With the needle angled slightly away from you, push the needle through the layers until you feel the tip of the needle beneath the quilt (Photograph 4).

When you feel the needle tip, slide your finger underneath the quilt toward you, pushing against the side of the needle to help return

it to the top. At the same time, with your top hand, roll the needle away from you. Gently push the needle forward and up through the quilt layers, until the amount of needle showing is the length you want the next stitch to be (Photograph 5).

Lift the eye of the needle with your thimble finger, positioning your thumb just ahead of the stitching. Rock the needle upward until it is almost perpendicular to the quilt top Photograph 6). Push down on the needle until you feel the tip beneath the quilt again.

Push the needle tip up to the top with your finger underneath the quilt and, at the same time, with your thimble finger, roll the eye of the needle down and forward to return the tip to the surface (Photograph 7).

Repeat this rock-and-roll motion until the needle is full. Then pull it away from the quilt top until the stitches are snug. Remember that uniformity of stitching is more important than size.

*continued*

## Machine Quilting

Quilting by machine is more than 100 years old, but until recent years it was considered a less-desirable means of finishing a fine quilt. Today, improved sewing machines and presser feet make it possible to create heirloom-quality quilts in hours instead of months.

Before you're even ready to practice, make sure your machine is in top working order and its tension is reliable. Clean and oil it before you begin. Clear the lint from the bobbin area after each empty bobbin and lightly oil the race, shuttle, and any other moving parts with a cotton swab or telescoping oil bottle. Clean the entire machine again after eight hours of sewing.

Set up a work space that provides a large, flat surface level with the machine's bed (throat plate) to keep the quilt well supported and flat. If possible, set up one table behind the machine and another to your left. Try to arrange the work space so the machine faces into a room and the quilt doesn't have to climb the wall.

Finally, choose a comfortable chair that allows you to look down on your work. This lets your arms relax at your sides instead of reaching.

## Straight Lines

To quilt long lines, such as in the ditch and grids, use a walking foot (see Photograph 8). (Designs with curves and corners require the free-motion technique described at right.) If you've never machine-quilted, start with a practice piece, such as a single block of simple squares or strips. Layer it with a thin cotton batting and a muslin backing; baste with safety pins.

Rather than backstitching, lock off stitches by setting the machine's stitch length to the shortest setting. Start the line on that setting, sewing forward about ¼". Then stop and reset the stitch length to 10 to 12 stitches per inch. Repeat this process at the beginning and end of every seam.

When working with a walking foot, start by sewing in the ditch of the quilt's lengthwise center seam, border to border. Turn the quilt crosswise, readjust the layers, and stitch the center crosswise seam. For small pieces, stitch all the lengthwise lines on one side of the center, then on the other side. Rotate the quilt and stitch the crosswise lines in the same manner.

For a large quilt, stitch all the lengthwise lines in the quadrant to the right of the lengthwise center seam. Turn the quilt 180° and stitch the lines in the diagonally opposite quadrant. Repeat the process in the remaining quadrants. Complete the grid by stitching crosswise lines in the same quadrant-by-quadrant order.

As you feed the fabric up to the walking foot, don't allow the foot to push fabric ahead. This causes tucks at the crossing of each seam. Give excess fabric to the foot, and allow it to ease the fabric into the seam evenly. Do not stretch or force the quilt top, as the batting and the finished quilt may become distorted.

## Free-Motion Quilting

Quilting with a walking foot is limited to straight lines. For curved patterns, including hand quilters' fancy designs, use a darning foot (see Photograph 9). This foot jumps up and down as the needle raises and lowers, allowing you to move the fabric freely while the needle is up, but holding the layers flat and compressed when the needle is taking a stitch.

Drop or cover the machine's feed dogs. You will manually control the stitch length, direction, and speed the fabric moves.

For practice, layer a piece of thin cotton batting between two pieces of muslin. Bring the bobbin thread to the surface of the fabric and hold both threads as you begin to stitch. When you press on the foot control, however, the fabric will stand still. You need to manually move it in the direction you wish to go. The speed you run the machine combined with the speed you move the fabric creates your stitch length. Practice to get a feel for this and to develop a consistent stitch length.

In the beginning, move the fabric slowly while running the machine at a medium-fast speed. Try to develop a rhythm with the motor while making scribbles on the fabric. Rather than turn the fabric, glide it in the direction it needs to go. Practice locking your stitches by moving the fabric very slowly, which creates minute stitches, for about ¼". This should be done at the beginning and end of every quilting line.

Once you've practiced for a while, select a small project to machine-quilt. A print fabric top will camouflage small glitches. Outline, echo, and stippling are good first project patterns. Stippling is a meandering, allover technique involving lines that do not touch, do not cross, do not have points, and are consistently spaced. Look beyond the hole in the darning foot and watch where you've been and where you are going.

Fancier patterns, such as feathers and cables, require advance planning to minimize the number of endings. When you're ready to tackle those patterns, stop at a quilt shop for a reference book.

Tying, or tufting, is a quick-and-easy alternative to quilting. It is an appropriate, useful finish for a quilt that will get a lot of wear and tear. Save fine stitching for a quilt that will be cared for and treasured.

Quilts that are tied have a puffier look than those that are quilted. For extra puffiness, use a thick batting or even multiple layers of batting. For an added touch, sew buttons or other colorful ornaments onto the quilt top as you tie.

The best materials for tying are perle cotton, sport-weight yarn, or narrow ribbon. A tie is a stitch taken through all three layers of the quilt and knotted on the surface of the quilt top. In some cases, the knot is on the back.

To make a tie, from the right side of the quilt top, make a single running stitch through all layers, leaving a 3" tail (see Diagram 1). Make a single backstitch through the same holes formed by the running stitch.

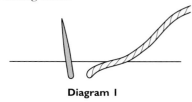

**Diagram 1**

Clip the thread, leaving a second 3" tail. Tie the clipped threads in a square knot close to the surface of the quilt (see Diagram 2). Don't pull the thread too tightly or it will create a pucker in the fabric.

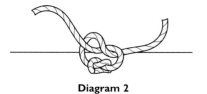

**Diagram 2**

# FINISHING

*The final step in quiltmaking is to bind the edges. Follow our easy instructions for a neat and durable edge on your quilt.*

The binding for most quilts is cut on the straight grain of the fabric. If your quilt has curved edges, cut the strips on the bias (see *page 149*). The cutting instructions for projects in this book specify the number of binding strips or a total length needed to finish the quilt. The instructions also specify enough width for a French-fold or double-layer binding because it's easier to apply and adds durability.

Join the strips with diagonal seams to make one continuous binding strip (see Diagram 1). Trim the excess fabric, leaving ¼" seam allowances. Press the seam allowances open.

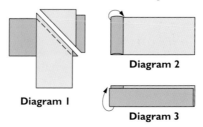

**Diagram 1**

**Diagram 2**

**Diagram 3**

Then, with the wrong sides together, fold under 1" at one end of the binding strip (see Diagram 2); press. Fold the strip in half lengthwise (see Diagram 3); press.

Beginning in the center of one side, place the binding strip against the right side of the quilt top, aligning the binding strip's raw edges with the quilt top's raw edge (see Diagram 4). Sew through all layers, stopping ¼" from the corner. Backstitch, then clip the threads. Remove the quilt from under the sewing-machine presser foot.

Fold the binding strip upward (see Diagram 5), creating a diagonal fold, and finger-press.

Holding the diagonal fold in place with your finger, bring the binding strip down in line with the next edge, making a horizontal fold that aligns with the top edge of the quilt (see Diagram 6).

Start sewing again at the top of the horizontal fold, stitching through all layers. Sew around the quilt, turning each corner in the same manner.

When you return to the starting point, lap the binding strip inside the beginning fold (see Diagram 7). Finish sewing to the starting point (see Diagram 8). Trim the batting and backing fabric even with the quilt top edges.

Turn the binding over the edge of the quilt to the back. Hand-stitch the binding to the backing fabric, making sure to cover any machine stitching.

To make mitered corners on the back, hand-stitch the binding up to a corner; fold a miter in the binding. Take a stitch or two in the fold to secure it. Then stitch the binding in place up to the next corner. Finish each corner in the same manner.

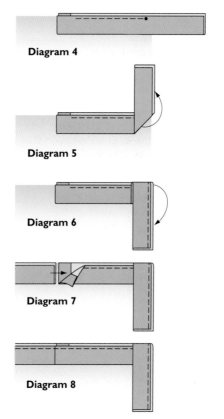

**Diagram 4**

**Diagram 5**

**Diagram 6**

**Diagram 7**

**Diagram 8**

# CREDITS

## Quilt Designers

**Alice Berg**
*Autumn Splendor*
Alice Berg of Marietta, Georgia, is one of three designers at Little Quilts. She enjoys replicating antique quilts.

**Cindy Blackberg and Mary Sorensen**
*Beauty Everlasting*
Cindy Blackberg (far left) of Sorrento, Florida, and Mary Sorensen of Longwood, Florida, enjoy team-teaching hand piecing and needle-turn appliqué.

**Christine Brown**
*Orient Express*
Christine Brown of Castle Rock, Colorado, collects specialty fabrics at quilt shops and quilt shows across the country.

**Marty Freed**
*Heaven & Earth*
Marty Freed of Winterset, Iowa, turns traditional blocks into finished quilts that her family enjoys using.

**Wendy Hager and Shirlene Fennema**
*Wheels of Whimsy*
Wendy Hager (far left) and Shirlene Fennema of Lake Forest, California, often collaborate on quilts. Wendy is the owner of Material Possessions Quilt Shop.

**Bettina Havig**
*English Elegance*
Bettina Havig of Columbia, Missouri, is the author of books on quilting, and has been teaching quilting for more than 20 years.

**Judith Hughes Marte**
*Love & a Little Lunacy*
Judith Hughes Marte of Nine Mile Falls, Washington, creates her own line—Around the Block Quilt Designs—of quilts, wall hangings and wearables.

**Jean Lepper**
*Christmas by Candlelight*
Jean Lepper of Redwood Falls, Minnesota, creates quilts with a warm and woodsy look. She is the owner of Main Street Cotton Quilt Shop in Redwood Falls and Hutchinson, Minnesota.

**Marjorie Levine**
*Town Square*
Marjorie Levine of Marietta, Georgia, finds the exchange of information a valuable part of belonging to the East Cobb Quilter's Guild.

**Marti Michell**
*Storm at Sea*
Marti Michell of Marietta, Georgia, teaches quiltmaking, writes books, designs patterns, and develops specialty tools for quilters.

**Cindy Taylor Oates**
*Toyland*
Cindy Taylor Oates of Phoenix, Arizona, develops her own line of patterns—Taylor Made Designs—and is one of three designers affiliated with The Redwork Club.

**Mabeth Oxenreider**
*Home & Beyond*
Mabeth Oxenreider of Carlisle, Iowa, teaches quilting classes on topics ranging from traditional blocks to watercolor quilts.

**Jill Reber**
*Stars Ablaze*
Jill Reber of Granger, Iowa, collaborated with her husband, Jim, to create Master Piece rulers and patterns for quilters.

**Laura Boehnke**
*New projects*
Laura Boehnke of Garner, Iowa, created all of the new projects shown in this book. She is the quilt tester for *American Patchwork & Quilting* magazine.

---

Thanks to Susan and Roger Petersen who graciously loaned a quilt made by Eleanor Sandholm.

### Project Quilters and Finishers
Karen Cary
Dawn Cavanaugh
Diane Ebner
Kathleen Pappas
Fern Stewart
Ruth A. Smith
Sally Terry

### Materials Suppliers
Bali Fabrics-Princess Mirah Designs
Benartex, Inc.
Chanteclaire
Clothworks, Fabric Sales Co.
David Textiles, Inc.
Fairfield Processing Co.
Patrick Lose for Hi-Fashion Fabrics, Inc.
Hoffman California Fabrics
In The Beginning Fabrics
June Tailor
Kent Avery
Maywood Studio
Mission Valley Textiles

Moda Fabrics
Northcott/Monarch
P&B Textiles
RJR Fashion Fabrics
Robert Kaufman Co., Inc.
Spectrix
Springs Industries, Inc.
Superior Threads, Inc.
YLI Corporation

### Watercolor Illustrations
Jan Gipple

### Photographers
**Marcia Cameron:** pages 12, 20, 24, 25, 44, 55, 69, 70, 89, 99, 101, 104, 105, 108, 114, 124, and 144
**Hopkins Associates:** pages 19, 22, 38, 40, 77, and 140
**Scott Little:** page 16
**Perry Struse:** pages 12, 13, 15, 19, 21, 26, 27, 29, 32, 34, 36, 37, 42, 43, 45, 46, 51, 53, 62, 67, 71, 73, 78, 80, 81, 82, 87, 90, 94, 96, 98, 103, 106, 107, 110, 120, 125, 127, 129, 133, 135, 137, and 143
**Steve Struse:** pages 8, 48, 51, 112, 115, 117, and 145